THE PARENTS' GUIDE TO
BODY DYSMORPHIC DISORDER

The Parents' Guide to Body Dysmorphic Disorder

How to Support Your Child, Teen or Young Adult

Nicole Schnackenberg,
Benedetta Monzani and Amita Jassi

Foreword by Rob Willson and David Veale

Jessica Kingsley Publishers
London and Philadelphia

First published in Great Britain in 2020 by Jessica Kingsley Publishers
An Hachette Company

2

A CIP catalogue record for this title is available from the British Library and the
Library of Congress

ISBN 978 1 78775 113 2
eISBN 978 1 78775 114 9

Printed and bound by CPI Group (UK) Ltd, Croydon CR0 4YY

Jessica Kingsley Publishers' policy is to use papers that are natural, renewable
and recyclable products and made from wood grown in sustainable forests.
The logging and manufacturing processes are expected to conform to the
environmental regulations of the country of origin.

Jessica Kingsley Publishers
73 Collier Street
London N1 9BE, UK

www.jkp.com

Contents

Acknowledgements

We would like to extend our gratitude to the trustees of the BDD Foundation for their support with this project, and for continuing to raise awareness and provide resources for people with BDD and their families. Special thanks go to OCD Action also.

We are indebted to Jessica Kingsley Publishers, particularly to Jane Evans and Madeleine Budd, for commissioning this book and for their belief in its importance and scope.

Our sincere thanks also to all those who made comments on the first draft of the book, particularly to Dr Sarah Sivers, educational psychologist, whose suggestions and comments enhanced the manuscript beyond measure.

Lastly, we are immensely grateful to all the young people and families who have inspired this book with their stories and tremendous courage. The greatest amount of thanks goes to the young people and families who have been involved in the writing and consultation of this book; we consider you to be our co-authors. The information contained herein has been immeasurably enriched by your experience, insight and wisdom. For that we cannot possibly thank you enough.

Foreword

Rob Willson and David Veale

We have now both been involved in the research and treatment of body dysmorphic disorder (BDD) for a quarter of a century. When we began, the term 'body dysmorphic disorder', or 'BDD', was rarely heard in mainstream psychiatry, let alone in general practice. Often, even if someone was given a diagnosis of BDD, they would be unlikely to be offered effective treatment. This book, offering clear practical advice to parents on how to support a young person with BDD, is a reflection of just how far the field has come. Not only do we now have a better understanding of BDD, and of how to treat the condition; we also have specialist services for both adults and young people in the UK.

BDD is best understood as a distressing and disabling pre-occupation with perceived defects or flaws in the appearance, usually lasting several hours a day. Individuals with BDD tend to check their appearance repeatedly and try to camouflage or alter the defects they are preoccupied with, frequently leading to demands for cosmetic and/or dermatological procedures. Parents are frequently perplexed because they can see nothing out of the ordinary in their child's appearance. They regularly tell us they feel frustrated that their attempts to reassure their child seem to fall on deaf ears. Causing significant anxiety and shame, BDD makes sufferers excessively self-conscious and often leads to substantial interference with their ability to function socially and educationally. This book responds to the needs of parents of young people with BDD who are often desperate for good information on what they should (and should not) do to best help their loved one.

It is important for parents to understand that their child's BDD is neither the child's fault nor their own. The causes of BDD are complex, and have yet to be fully unravelled. What we do know is that it is possible for parents to set helpful conditions for their child to recover and that there are certain reliable do's-and-don'ts that support change. One of the key aspects is to understand that BDD is a product of an overloaded brain. The young person with BDD simply cannot see the wood for the trees; they are unable to see their appearance objectively, no matter how many times they are 'told' or reassured that they look okay. It is only as their preoccupation (and therefore brain-overload) decreases that their objectivity can return. It may seem like a small thing when dealing with such a big issue but avoiding the trap of getting bogged down in repeated and unproductive conversations about appearance can be very helpful. A parent who never loses sight of the wider interests and attributes of their child can be a great asset. Even a few minutes of engaging the young person externally away from their appearance concerns can be helpful. Each minute stolen away from appearance preoccupation and diverted into the outside world is a small but significant victory.

The authors of this parents' guide to BDD are experts on BDD in young people and the advice given here is rounded by many years of experience. Schnackenberg, Monzani and Jassi guide the reader through a journey of BDD diagnosis and treatment. They advise on how to respond to their loved one's BDD-driven behaviours, as well as managing the impact and mood difficulties that typically accompany BDD.

The authors give helpful advice on supporting a young person and working with teachers on how to help the young person to succeed in their education. While aimed at parents, the content of this book will be highly relevant to friends, partners, siblings and anyone who cares for a young person with BDD. Chapter 6 has particular relevance for educational professionals.

In this book, you will find crucial guidance on finding the correct help – for many, this is one of the most difficult steps on the road to recovery. There is also advice about supporting a young person through psychological and medical treatment. Contemporary issues regarding managing a young person's use of social media are also addressed.

Having a child with BDD can be an extremely strenuous experience for parents. Helpfully, advice can be found for parents within these pages on how to look after their own wellbeing as well as the wellbeing of their loved one.

Of particular note are the contributions in this book from parents who have first-hand experience of taking care of a child or young person with BDD, and from young people with BDD themselves about their lived experience. 'Real life' experience of living with, and ultimately breaking free from, BDD is vastly helpful to others. We thank these contributors for offering hope, encouragement and advice to parents going through a very challenging time.

Introduction

Body dysmorphic disorder (BDD) most commonly emerges in the adolescent years and can have a devastating impact on families. Parents and carers typically bear much of the burden. Parents often tell us they feel confused about why BDD came into their child's life, what BDD is and isn't, how to talk about BDD with both their child and others, and how to access and support their child through treatment. Other common struggles parents share include difficulties with supporting their child through education; navigating their child's requests for physical treatments such as cosmetic surgery, dentistry and dermatology; and taking care of themselves and other family members when swept away by the demands and emotional turmoil BDD can bring.

We understand the tremendous challenges that come along with being a parent of a child or young person struggling with BDD. We have written this book to both offer practical support and guidance and to help you to know that you are not alone in your experiences.

The information in these pages will be relevant to you whether or not your child has received an official diagnosis of BDD.

This book can be read at various stages of the journey, including before, during and after treatment has been accessed. Chapter 7 covers seeking treatment for BDD, including how you can support your child while awaiting such treatment. Chapter 8 addresses supporting your child through the treatment itself, including how you can be a recovery agent in this process.

This book has been written in such a way that it is possible to dip in and out of the various chapters depending on what you require support with at any given time. However, we recommend you ideally read the first four chapters before going into the others as they offer an overview of what BDD is, how BDD can affect the young person and those supporting them, common struggles that go alongside the experience of BDD and considerations of how to respond to various BDD-related behaviours. These topics offer a foundation for the subject areas covered in subsequent chapters.

Some of the chapters may feel rather difficult to read; particularly, perhaps, Chapter 5 which covers coping with low mood and hopelessness. You might find it helpful to read emotionally evocative chapters alongside other trusted family members or close friends so you can share the thoughts and feelings that arise as a result. Dipping into Chapter 10, which covers self-care for parents, is recommended if you are feeling strongly affected by the content in any of the other chapters.

There is a fair amount of subject-related vocabulary for BDD, particularly when it comes to thinking about treatment. We have included a Glossary of Terms, which you can find at the back of the book, to aid your understanding of any unfamiliar concepts. We hope this shall be supportive to your experience of reading this book.

In addition to the resources and ideas offered in the main body of the text, we have also included various helplines and avenues of support in the Resources section at the back of the book, including some further reading which may be of interest to you. We particularly wish to highlight the online support group for parents of young people with BDD run by OCD Action.[1] This group takes place over Skype and can, therefore, be accessed from any geographical area.

It is our sincere wish that this book will serve as a relevant and practical resource for you as you navigate the vicissitudes of supporting a child or young person with BDD. As you will read, particularly in Chapter 11 in which four parents share their stories, and in Chapter 12 which considers building a life beyond BDD, there is always hope. Please hold in mind as you read this book that, with the right support and treatment, many young people find their way beyond their struggles with BDD and go on to live enjoyable and fulfilling lives.

---

[1] www.ocdaction.org.uk/support-group/bdd-parents-skypephone-support-group

CHAPTER 1

What Is Body Dysmorphic Disorder?

In this chapter we will look at how body dysmorphic disorder (BDD) typically manifests itself in children and young people (referred to in the rest of this book as *young people* for ease of reading). We will explore the diagnostic criteria and consider other mental health conditions that go alongside BDD for some young people.

Young people with a diagnosis of BDD believe they have defects or flaws in their appearance which make them abnormal or 'ugly' in some way. Words young people with BDD have used to describe themselves to us have included 'hideous', 'disgusting', 'monstrous', 'sub-human' and 'deformed'. In BDD, the young person's perceived defects either cannot be seen by others or are viewed by the outside eye as part of normal human variation.

Young people with BDD may be focused on literally any aspect of their appearance, although a distressing preoccupation with the skin, hair, teeth and nose are some of the most commonly reported areas of concern. Some young people will be focused on one aspect of their appearance at any given time, while others may be fixated on multiple aspects at the same time.

Young people with BDD are excessively preoccupied with their perceived appearance flaws to such an extent that they experience significant emotional distress and can find it challenging to continue with their usual activities of daily living. For example, some young people find it difficult to go to school or college, to concentrate on tasks, to socialize, or even to leave the house.

Young people with BDD engage in repetitive behaviours in an attempt to fix or hide what they think is wrong with their appearance. Some examples of compulsive and repetitive behaviours related to BDD include mirror checking (and spending long periods of time, sometimes many hours a day, 'stuck' looking in the mirror), reassurance seeking, camouflaging, skin picking, compulsively seeking dermatology/dentistry/cosmetic surgery, continually touching the perceived defect, adhering to a rigid diet, and/or covering up windows/mirrors/reflective surfaces among others.

The extent to which young people have insight into the fact that BDD is psychological in nature varies from young person to young person. Often young people with a diagnosis of BDD have a poor level of insight into their situation, that is, they believe the perceived defect to be real and cannot recognize that the level of their distress is significantly disproportionate. As one young person explained to us:

> 'I was very much in denial that I had BDD, like viciously in denial until about a few months ago honestly. In my head I'd say to myself, "If my skin was fine, I'd be completely fine so it can't be BDD."'

Although less is known about BDD than many other mental health diagnoses, it is significantly more common than many people believe and it affects an estimated 2.2 per cent of the UK adolescent population and between 2 and 3 per cent of the general population. This makes BDD more prevalent than better-understood conditions such as anorexia and schizophrenia. BDD affects males and females almost equally and can emerge at any age, although in the majority of cases it begins in the adolescent years.

There are many crossovers between BDD and other mental health diagnoses including depression, social anxiety disorder, obsessive compulsive disorder (OCD), eating disorders and body-focused repetitive behaviours such as compulsive skin-picking (excoriation) disorder and hair-pulling (trichotillomania) disorder. It is possible to have a diagnosis of BDD alongside another mental health diagnosis, with anxiety and depression being the most common of these.

Importantly, whilst the focus of attention in BDD is on the physical appearance, BDD is not about vanity in any way. Rather, BDD would appear to have its foundations in a lack of self-worth, a poor self-concept, and a chronically low self-esteem. As one young person explained to us:

> 'I was always striving not to be pretty, not to be attractive, not to be good looking but to be a little less hideous so it was tolerable for other people. I think that's what people sometimes misunderstand about BDD. They think it's something to do with vanity or narcissism or something but, oh gosh, that couldn't be further from the truth, I don't think.'

Another young person told us:

> 'I think a lot of people hear that BDD is about appearance and think, well, what's so bad about that? You know, just get over it, kind of thing. But BDD affects you in sort of all aspects of your life. It definitely does impact everything I do really.'

In the most recent edition of the *Diagnostic and Statistical Manual of Mental Disorders* (DSM-V) the following criteria are given for a diagnosis of BDD:

BDD diagnosis criteria

- *Appearance preoccupations*: the young person is preoccupied with one or more perceived defects or flaws in their physical appearance. 'Preoccupation' is usually classified as thinking about the perceived defects for at least an hour a day, but it is typically much more than this.
- *Repetitive behaviours*: at some point, the young person performs repetitive, compulsive behaviours in response to their appearance concerns. These compulsions can be behavioural and thus observed by others – for example, mirror checking, excessive grooming, skin picking, reassurance seeking, or clothes changing. Other BDD compulsions are mental acts – such as comparing one's appearance with that of other people.
- *Clinical significance*: the preoccupation causes

---

clinically significant distress or difficulties in the young person's social, occupational or other important areas of functioning.

- *Differentiation from an eating disorder:* if the appearance preoccupations focus on being too fat or weighing too much, the clinician may diagnose an eating disorder. However, concerns with fat or weight in a young person of normal weight can be a symptom of BDD. It is not uncommon to have both an eating disorder and BDD.

- *Specifiers:* DSM-V also includes two specifiers (specifiers are extensions to a diagnosis to further clarify a condition or illness):
  - Muscle dysmorphia: muscle dysmorphia is a form of BDD whereby the young person is preoccupied with concerns that his or her body build is too small or insufficiently muscular.
  - Insight specifier: this specifier indicates the degree of insight regarding BDD beliefs which can be classified as good, fair or poor.

BDD can be very confusing for both young people and families. It can be particularly perplexing for the young person as, in the early stages, they often conceptualize their 'issue' as being physical and not emotional/psychological in nature. While family members and clinical professionals might be wondering about or suggesting a diagnosis of BDD, the young person themselves may believe that once their perceived appearance defect(s) are 'fixed', everything will be okay.

Young people with a diagnosis of BDD sometimes find it difficult to understand why psychological treatment will be of any help to them. Rather, they might feel that what is needed is a dentist, a cosmetic surgeon, a dermatologist or someone similar – not a psychologist, psychiatrist or counsellor.

At other times, the young person may themselves recognize that they are struggling with BDD before any family members or professionals have put a name to their distress. Sometimes, a young person will oscillate between believing they have something called BDD and may, therefore, require psychological help and feeling convinced that they have a physical defect that needs 'fixing' in some way.

Muscle dysmorphia

Muscle dysmorphia is a sub-type of BDD. Muscle dysmorphia is characterized by the belief that one's body is too small or insufficiently muscular or 'puny'. Behaviours associated with muscle dysmorphia include spending extensive time at the gym (even when severely fatigued or injured), extensive mirror checking, camouflaging, maintaining a diet low in fat and high in protein, and the use of nutritional supplements and anabolic-androgenic steroids. Although muscle dysmorphia is typically associated with males, it can occur in females also. Muscle dysmorphia can have catastrophic physical consequences including kidney failure, heart disease and musculoskeletal injuries.

Young people with muscle dysmorphia can find it particularly difficult to accept that they are struggling with a mental health condition as exercise and low-fat diets are held up societally as being both healthy and commendable. As with BDD, it can help to support the young person to consider the negative impact their preoccupations and behaviours are having on their day-to-day life, that is, to recognize the significant impairment in daily functioning, which is indicative of a mental health struggle.

How do I know if my child has BDD?

Only a trained mental health professional can make a clinical diagnosis of BDD. However, there are various screening tools freely available which might help you to figure out if your child might be struggling with BDD. Sometimes, young people complete these screening tools at home and then print them out to share with their GP, psychiatrist, etc. We recommend the Body Dysmorphic Disorder Questionnaire (BDDQ) for adolescents, the Appearance Anxiety Inventory (AAI) and/or the Body Dysmorphic Disorder modification of the Yale-Brown Obsessive-Compulsive Disorder Scale for Adolescents (BDD Y-BOCS), which are scientifically validated tools. Screening measures can be accessed on the BDD Foundation website.[1] Of course, there are also young people who self-identify as having BDD without ever receiving a formal diagnosis.

Please note that your child does not need to be presenting with all of the following points to be experiencing BDD, but some other important considerations might be:

- Is the amount my child is looking in the mirror/avoiding

---

[1] https://bddfoundation.org/helping-you/questionnaires

the mirror considerably greater than most other young people I know?

- Does my child compulsively check their perceived defect in reflective surfaces such as windows, metal implements, etc.?

- Are you unable to see the perceived defect your child is distressed about, or do you perceive it as part of normal human variation? For example, your child says they have severe acne, but you view their skin as being in line with other adolescents their age.

- Is your child experiencing considerable emotional distress related to their perceived defect?

- Does your child believe that when their perceived flaw is 'fixed' or improved, their emotional distress will reduce? For example, do they say things like, 'When my skin clears up, everything will be okay'?

- Is your child's perceived defect making it more difficult to engage, or stopping them from engaging, in their usual activities of daily living? These might be, for example, going out with their friends, going to school/college/ university, engaging in hobbies, going to the shop for groceries, having their hair cut.

- Does your child try to camouflage (hide or cover up) their perceived flaw using cosmetics, clothing, hair, etc.?

- Does your child spend time each week researching cosmetic surgeons, dermatologists, dentists, etc.?

- Does your child sometimes talk about a sense of hopelessness because their perceived defect is so distressing to them?

- Does your child avoid certain lighting, avoid speaking

to people from certain angles, etc. for fear that their perceived defect will be magnified?

- Does your child avoid certain everyday tasks for fear of making their perceived defect worse? For example, does your child avoid touching bath towels to their face for fear of causing skin blemishes, or avoid eating certain foods for fear of making their teeth yellow?
- Does your child compulsively compare their body, or parts of their body to others'?
- Does your child seek continuous reassurance about their appearance from others? Or do they avoid engaging in any appearance-related discussion for fear that they will draw attention to their perceived defect?
- Does your child assume that others think they are ugly? Hideous?
- Does your child feel compelled to spend hours in the gym when they would rather be somewhere else? Do they take steroids in an attempt to increase their musculature? Do they follow a certain diet (e.g. high protein) in order to increase or maintain their musculature, even if they don't enjoy it or it doesn't make them feel good physically?

What BDD is not

It is important to be clear on what BDD is *not*, so we can best recognize what it is. This is also important in terms of ensuring your child's experiences are not missed or minimized in any way.

For certain, BDD has nothing to do with vanity. As BDD most typically emerges in adolescence (although it can also emerge before or after this period), sometimes it gets put down to 'normal' teenage appearance anxieties. This is, to some degree, understandable as many teens do indeed spend some time feeling concerned about aspects of their appearance. However, BDD is different. In BDD, the young person's appearance-related preoccupation is so intense and distressing that it prevents them from living life in the way they typically would. Young people with BDD are certainly not vain and tell us that they are desperately attempting to achieve an appearance that is simply 'normal' and 'acceptable' – they are not striving after beauty or perfection in its most commonly understood sense. As one young person shared with us when asked to describe BDD:

> 'It's not vanity. It's not a normal dissatisfaction with the appearance – a lot of people would say everyone has that. It's a mental problem that causes an impact on daily functioning.'

Given that BDD has nothing to do with vanity, positive comments about your child's appearance may not be believed by them or may backfire. Therefore, many parents tell us that it is beneficial to completely refrain from commenting on their child's appearance when they are struggling with BDD. One young person shared the following with us, which is something we hear quite a lot:

> 'I remember my whole attitude to whenever my family, especially my mum, were trying to say something nice, almost complimentary. I have these memories...like I had come downstairs ready to go out or something with my friend

and my Mum would go, "Oh, you look nice" and I'd be like, "How dare you lie to me like that?" and be really defensive.'

BDD is also different from eating disorders like anorexia, although the two diagnoses can overlap. In eating disorders, the concern is about gaining weight or being too fat, leading the person to engage in unhealthy behaviours to limit or control weight and body size. Whilst a young person with BDD may be restricting their food intake, the purpose of their behaviour may not be about changing their weight but rather related to changing the appearance of a particular body part. For example, some young people with BDD restrict their food intake in order to change the shape of their face. Others may restrict their diet to specific foods in order to keep their skin clear, to thicken their hair, to increase their musculature and so on.

It is also important to note that BDD is sometimes put down to social worries. Indeed, some young people receive diagnoses like social anxiety disorder before clinicians realize their appearance-focused distress is the reason for their social avoidance. It is important to get to the bottom of the reasons why a young person is avoiding social situations and for these reasons to be targeted in treatment.

Diagnoses commonly associated with BDD

Psychiatric diagnoses like BDD are rarely clear-cut. The diagnosis of BDD is made by a mental health clinician, based on an observable set of behaviours, which doctors often call 'symptoms'. Symptoms associated with BDD are also associated with other psychiatric diagnoses. Therefore, your child may have received other diagnoses prior to their diagnosis of BDD or may be diagnosed with other conditions alongside their diagnosis of BDD. The psychiatric labels explored in the following suggestions are not an exhaustive list but contain some of the most common diagnoses that overlap with BDD.

Depression

Depression has been found to be correlated with BDD in many research studies and is characterized by persistent and life-affecting low mood. Doctors must rule out depression from medical causes (such as vitamin deficiencies and medication) before a diagnosis of a primary depressive mood disorder can be made.

It is important to note that children younger than seven years old may have a limited ability to communicate negative emotions and thoughts with language. They may, therefore, 'somatize' their experiences, experiencing negative emotions like sadness as physical symptoms such as general aches and pains, headaches and stomach aches. Ruling out biological causes for these physical experiences is, again, important before a diagnosis of depression can be considered.

The feelings of hopelessness connected with depression can be linked to the perceived defect(s) in young people experiencing BDD. For example, the young person may feel they are depressed as a result of their distressing preoccupation with their perceived appearance defect. Importantly, low mood can also precede any focus on the appearance. Sometimes, young people can unconsciously 'blame' their perceived defect for making them feel sad/confused/shameful, etc. For example, a young person may come to believe the reason they feel so sad is because their skin is blemished; and that they will no longer feel so sad when their skin clears up. This kind of thinking pattern can lead the young person into a self-amplifying cycle of trying to feel better by changing/'fixing' aspects of their physical appearance, only to find that they still feel incredibly sad.

Feelings of hopelessness are common features of both depression and BDD. This can be particularly frightening for young people and for their parents and families. We will look more at how to support your child if they are experiencing feelings of hopelessness in Chapter 5.

Anxiety disorders

'BDD wasn't my first diagnosis. I first had anxiety and OCD and then later, when I went up to high school, it kind of became BDD.'

(A young person with BDD)

Anxiety is characterized by persistent, irrational and overwhelming fear or worry that interferes with daily living.

In one sense, anxiety is a normal part of childhood (and adulthood also). Every young person goes through phases of anxiety. These phases are temporary and rarely impact significantly on a young person's life. Anxiety becomes a diagnosable mental health condition, however, when a young person experiences persistent anxiety which impacts on their ability to enjoy and engage fully in their lives.

Anxiety-related experiences you might notice in your child can include panic attacks, unexplainable nausea/headaches/ stomach aches, etc., repeated nightmares, constant reassurance seeking and excessive shyness. Anxiety and depression can go hand in hand for some young people. You might notice that your child is hyper-aroused (hyper-active and anxious) at times and hypo-aroused (fatigued and depressed) at other times. Anxiety is fundamentally part of BDD. BDD, in fact, is considered to be an anxiety disorder. Any treatment for BDD, therefore, should target the anxiety element of your child's experience alongside other aspects. To read more about support for anxiety as an element of treatment for BDD, please see Chapter 8.

Social anxiety disorder

Forty per cent of BDD sufferers also meet diagnostic criteria for social anxiety disorder (SAD). Whilst BDD and SAD do often co-occur, it has also been reported that BDD can be easily mis-diagnosed as SAD, given their similarities. SAD is characterized by intense self-consciousness and fear of embarrassment that goes beyond typical shyness, causing a young person to go to great lengths to avoid social interactions. Sometimes, this might lead to agoraphobia (fear and avoidance of social situations). If your child's social anxiety is connected to their perceived appearance flaw and a fear of judgement from others because of their appearance concerns, this may indicate that they are struggling with BDD and not SAD.

Obsessive compulsive disorder (OCD)

BDD is closely related to OCD in terms of diagnostic criteria, as both conditions come under the umbrella of 'obsessive com-pulsive and related disorders' in DSM-5. OCD is characterized by the presence of obsessions and compulsions. Obsessions are defined by recurrent and persistent thoughts, urges or impulses that are experienced, at some time during the disturbance, as intrusive and unwanted. In most cases, these obsessions cause the young person marked anxiety and/or distress. The young person attempts to ignore or suppress these thoughts, urges, etc. by performing a repetitive behaviour or mental act they feel driven to perform, with the aim of reducing their anxiety and/or distress. Again, if your child's obsessions and preoccupations are related specifically to their perceived appearance defect(s), they may receive a diagnosis of BDD rather than OCD.

Anorexia/bulimia/binge-eating disorder/orthorexia/ Other Specified Feeding or Eating Disorders (OSFED)

It is not uncommon for young people with a diagnosis of BDD to experience food-related distress. Young people with a diagnosis of BDD may restrict their food intake, purge what they have eaten, exercise to excess and other related practices in order to alter the shape and form of parts of their body. As one young person explained to us:

> 'Trying to control my weight was the only way without undergoing invasive surgery that I could manipulate the shape of my face. Some people might be more focused on like the size of their waist or the number on the scales but for me, above all, it was how my face looked at different stages of weight loss and weight gain.'

Typically, a diagnosis of BDD is not given if the main focus of your child's attention is on altering the overall weight of their body. In this instance, they would be more likely to receive an eating disorder diagnosis. If your child's restrictive/compulsive eating behaviours are focused on changing specific parts of their body (e.g. skin, face, hair), however, they may be more likely to receive a diagnosis of BDD.

Sadly, disordered eating behaviours go hand in hand with BDD for a proportion of young people. We cannot emphasize strongly enough how important it is to take your child along to the GP as soon as possible if you believe they may be restricting their food intake or purging away what they have eaten. It is necessary to hold in mind that a young person does not need to be at a low body weight in order to be in physical danger from disordered eating as complications like heart arrhythmias, bone density changes and electrolyte imbalances can also occur at any weight, including at weights the Body Mass Index (BMI) charts deem to be healthy.

Trichotillomania and skin-picking (excoriation) disorder

Trichotillomania (hair-pulling disorder) is characterized by recurrent hair pulling from one's head or body resulting in significant hair loss despite repeated attempts to stop or decrease the hair-pulling behaviours. When the hair removal is intended to improve perceived defects in the appearance of body or facial hair, BDD is likely be diagnosed either alongside or rather than trichotillomania.

Skin-picking (excoriation) disorder is characterized by compulsive picking of the skin causing distress and/or impairment and resulting in skin lesions. When the skin picking is intended to improve perceived defects in the appearance of one's skin, BDD is likely to be diagnosed alongside or rather than dermatillomania/excoriation (skin-picking) disorder. One young person with a diagnosis of BDD who also regularly engaged in skin-picking explained the reasons for her picking to us in the following way:

> 'I would pick at my skin to get rid of blemishes or marks. That would obviously then make more marks and would break the skin, making it all red. I would sort of go into a trance-like state and could be stuck in the mirror for a few hours even. I remember my mum would say, "I can't see anything. You know, you're not actually picking anything – there's nothing there."'

A few, less common, diagnoses that can precede, come alongside or follow BDD include olfactory reference syndrome (ORS), substance use disorder and delusional disorder.

Olfactory reference syndrome (ORS)

ORS is characterized by a preoccupation with emitting a foul or unpleasant body odour. Although young people with ORS believe that they really do smell bad, other people cannot detect the odour. ORS usually triggers excessive, repetitive behaviours such as repeatedly checking oneself for body odour, excessively laundering one's clothes and excessive perfume/cologne use.

Substance use disorder

This is characterized by excessive use of alcohol and/or use of non-prescription drugs and other mind-altering substances. This includes taking the substance in larger amounts or for longer than one is meant to; wanting to reduce use of the substance but feeling unable to do so; cravings and urges to use the substance; and the substance having an impact on emotional health and wellbeing, activities of daily living and relationships.

Delusional disorder

This disorder is characterized by hallucinations and delusions, without the presence of psychotic symptoms, that have been present for at least a month. Delusions are false beliefs based on incorrect inferences about external reality that persist despite the evidence to the contrary. These beliefs are not ordinarily accepted by other members of the young person's culture or sub-culture.

Why is my child struggling with BDD?

Parents of young people with a diagnosis of BDD are generally desperate to understand why their child has BDD. This desperation is completely understandable. Unfortunately, it is still unclear exactly why young people end up struggling with BDD. There is typically a complex array of inter-linking factors that lead a young person to feel distressed about perceived defects in their appearance. It is not the case that a singular biological nuance, event, relationship, or anything else, is ever solely to 'blame'. Therefore, any guilt you may feel that you 'caused' your child's BDD in some way, as some parents tell us they feel, is very much unfounded. We want to give parents the clear message that BDD is NOT your fault and that you can be a very vital agent in your child's recovery.

Evolutionary factors

There is some evidence that young people with a diagnosis of BDD are more orientated towards perceived social threats in their environment. In evolutionary terms, it is adaptive to be vigilant towards potential attack/rejection in order to keep one's self safe. A young person's attempts to 'fix' aspects of their physical appearance, and their hyper-vigilance to how others may perceive their appearance, could be understood as an attempt to keep themselves safe from rejection and exclusion.

Genetics and neurochemistry

We still have a long way to go in terms of understanding the role of genetics in BDD. We know from some studies that around 8 per cent of people with a diagnosis of BDD have a family member who also has a diagnosis of BDD, which is a rate four to eight times higher than in the general population (Bienvenu et al., 2000). Twin studies have consistently surmised that this familiarity is mostly attributable to genetic factors (Enander et al., 2018, López-Solà et al., 2014, Monzani et al., 2012a, Monzani et al., 2012b).

BDD is thought to be causally linked to OCD, with studies showing a considerable genetic overlap between these conditions. This explains why BDD and OCD often co-occur and why BDD is more prevalent among first-degree relatives of people with OCD than among relatives of people without OCD. While there are a handful of studies suggesting that BDD shares genetic liability with OCD (Browne et al., 2014; López-Solà et al., 2014;

Monzani *et al.*, 2012b; Monzani *et al.*, 2014) and that genes predisposing someone to BDD are likely to be the same as the ones predisposing someone to OCD, specific genes have not yet been identified.

As you will read about in more detail later in Chapter 7, the two main treatment options recommended for BDD are cognitive behavioural therapy (CBT) and selective serotonin reuptake inhibitors (SSRIs). SSRIs are prescribed on account of serotonin's perceived role in BDD. Serotonin is most commonly believed to be a neurotransmitter which relays signals between nerve cells, or neurons, regulating their intensity. Neurochemical studies in BDD suggest that serotonin might play a role in BDD; SSRIs work by increasing levels of serotonin. One study, for example, found decreased serotonin binding densities in people with BDD when compared with healthy controls (Marazziti, Dell'Osso and Presta, 1999). This suggests that serotonin, the 'feel good hormone', may be taken up differently in the brains of people diagnosed with BDD.

Visual processing differences

There is some evidence to suggest that people with BDD process visual information differently (Beilharz *et al.*, 2017, Feusner *et al.*, 2007; Feusner *et al.*, 2010; Feusner *et al.*, 2011) and may present with higher levels of aestheticality, meaning they are more orientated towards pleasure through the visual sense. The findings of some research studies have suggested that people diagnosed with BDD may process visual information locally (Beilharz *et al.*, 2017; Feusner *et al.*, 2007; Feusner *et al.*, 2011; Jefferies, Laws and Fineberg, 2012) as opposed to globally. They home in and focus on the small details of visual information as opposed to processing the 'big picture'. Young people with BDD may, therefore, process aspects of their appearance as separate, composite parts as opposed to processing, for example, the face or body as a whole. This may lead them to notice nuances that are either unperceivable or only mildly perceivable (and put down to typical human variation) to the outside eye, such as asymmetric facial features, tiny blemishes and so on. Again, whether these visual processing differences predate the distressing preoccupation with the perceived defect or emerge as a result of it is unknown.

Personality traits and self-concept

BDD tends to go hand in hand with low self-esteem, a poor self-concept and perfectionistic tendencies. Young people with BDD often talk about having low self-esteem and being uncertain about their self-worth and place in the world prior to their appearance-related distress. Young people with BDD often describe their feelings of low self-worth as being broader than their appearance. This can exist alongside perfectionistic tendencies. As one young person with BDD put it:

'It is not just about appearance and it would sort of affect me and everything I did. Anything I did wasn't good enough and I just sort of felt like a bad person deep down.'

Another young person with BDD explained:

'I just felt very terrible about myself and I didn't feel like I had anything to offer anyone.'

Difficult life experiences

A high proportion of young people with BDD have had challenging life experiences such as teasing, bullying and difficult relationships (with family members, teachers and/or peers). These experiences exist on a continuum, ranging from the mildly upsetting to the deeply traumatic. Some young people diagnosed with BDD will not be able to recall any difficult life experiences at all.

Studies have found that young people with BDD are more likely to have experienced bullying than the general population (e.g. Neziroglu *et al.*, 2018; Weingarden *et al.*, 2017). This includes bullying focused on physical appearance and more generalized bullying episodes. These bullying and teasing experiences have been found to impact on young people's self-esteem, self-confidence and self-concept. It has been suggested by some BDD researchers that the young person then turns their attention to 'fixing' their perceived defect in order to negate future bullying experiences and avoid experiences of rejection.

Some studies of adults diagnosed with BDD have indicated that people with this diagnosis are more likely to have experienced childhood trauma: an experience of feeling under threat, and of one's emotional resources being overwhelmed, while being unable to fight back or escape in any way (e.g. Buhlmann, Marques and Wilhelm, 2012; Didie *et al.*, 2006; Neziroglu, Khemlani-Patel and Yaryura-Tobias, 2006). Such traumas might include bullying experiences, family mental health difficulties and/or conflict and the experience of acute academic pressure either from themselves or others.

It is very important to highlight the fact that BDD is never caused by one single person or factor. No one person or event is ever to blame for BDD. Rather, difficult life experiences are non-specific risk factors that may contribute to a young person's propensity to develop BDD. All the factors need to be considered when planning treatment and models of support.

There is still a long way to go in our understanding of BDD. More research is needed before we can say for certain why some young people experience BDD and others do not. However, research into BDD has increased considerably over the past decade and we are now armed with much more information and resources related to how to support young people to move beyond BDD and live an enjoyable and fulfilling life. As a parent, you have a vital part to play in this recovery process and it is our hope that the information in this book will support you in this endeavour.

CHAPTER 2

Responding to Common Behaviours in BDD

In this chapter we will consider how you can helpfully respond to different aspects of your child's BDD. We hope this chapter will increase your understanding of why your child may be behaving in certain ways and empower you to confidently come alongside them as a support and recovery agent.

Young people with BDD are excessively preoccupied with perceived flaws in their appearance and therefore engage in repetitive behaviours, or safety behaviours, in an attempt to 'fix' their perceived defect and reduce their distress. Every young person with BDD is different, though may share behaviours and preoccupations in common with other BDD sufferers. Coming to know and recognize each of the aspects of BDD can help parents to separate the young person out from their diagnosis and to elucidate ways of helpfully responding. Here are a few of the more common behaviours you might notice, and some ideas of how you may choose to respond to these.

It is important to note that young people will have different levels of insight into their BDD-related behaviours. What this means is that some young people will be able to see that their

BDD-related behaviours are detrimental to their wellbeing, whereas others may struggle to see that their behaviours are fuelling their distress at all. The suggestions in this chapter, therefore, may be taken up more willingly by some young people than others. Please do not feel disheartened if your strategies for supporting your child to move beyond their BDD-related behaviours are not successful straight away. Increasing insight into one's behaviours, and changing these behaviours, can take time and much repetition. Seeking professional support in this endeavour is strongly recommended.

Mirror checking and/or mirror avoidance

Some young people with a diagnosis of BDD engage in lengthy mirror gazing, while others avoid mirrors as much as possible, sometimes covering up or removing mirrors in order to avoid the distress of seeing their perceived defect. Mirror checking and mirror gazing in BDD tend to increase feelings of anxiety, shame and distress, particularly in the long term.

It might be difficult for you to know whether your child is spending long periods of time in front of the mirror, as mirror checking and lengthy periods of mirror gazing can be secretive and largely hidden. You might notice that your child is spending extended periods of time in the bathroom or in their bedroom, alone. You might also notice your child checking their appearance in other reflective surfaces like shop windows, the back of cutlery and so on. Some young people carry hand-held mirrors around with them all the time and become distressed if they cannot have access to them or cannot use them as often as they would like.

If your child is a mirror-avoider, you may notice they turn mirrors around, cover them up or walk past them with their eyes closed or head down. Some young people with BDD seek out specific mirrors and avoid others. You might notice that your child has certain 'safe' mirrors they like to look in, while avoiding others at all costs.

Checking and/or avoiding mirrors is a type of 'safety behaviour'. However, neither mirror gazing nor mirror avoidance tend to induce the feelings of safety the young person is seeking. Rather, spending a long time gazing at a perceived defect tends to magnify its felt impression, making it even more prominent in the young person's mind. Similarly, avoiding mirrors can lead to the belief that the perceived defect is worse than its reflection would suggest.

It can be very difficult to challenge young people about their use of the mirror. If you take mirrors away without your child's agreement, they will likely find other reflective surfaces to check themselves in. Likewise, if you uncover concealed mirrors without your child's consent, they will likely strive to find alternative means of avoiding their reflection, such as avoiding rooms within which mirrors and other reflective surfaces are present.

The first step in addressing your child's mirror use is to take an open, non-judgemental, curious and empathetic stance. This stance, in fact, is recommended as a first line of response to any safety behaviour your child is engaging in. You will be more likely to be met with a defensive response if you jump into opinions and solutions straight away. Make a relational connection with your child, such as through a kind word and a reassuring hand on their shoulder if they are willing to accept it, before you breach the subject of mirror gazing/avoidance with them. Avoid entering into any conflict or argument with your child, as this will be likely to increase their defensiveness and sense of isolation. Rather, express your empathy in whichever way feels natural to you, for example:

☐ I have noticed you are spending a long time in the bathroom, Jane. You seem to look quite upset when you come out. I am so sorry you feel that way. Whatever you are doing in the bathroom must be difficult for you. I am here to listen to what your time in the bathroom is like for you, if you would like to share.

☐ I have noticed you have covered up the mirror in the bathroom, Simon. I am so sorry if things are tricky for you right now. I wonder what it feels like for you?

Once you have connected through empathy with your child, you will have enabled them to feel seen, validated and understood. This should help to reduce any sense of shame they might be feeling. Having connected with compassion and empathy, you can then move into a solution-focused response, including considering practical tactics for dealing with the distress caused by the behaviour. As much as possible, try to stay with the experiences and suggestions of your child, as opposed to jumping in too soon with lots of ideas of your own of possible solutions. You might follow up the initial part of your discussion with something like:

☐ Thank you for sharing something about your experiences with me, Jane. You have been so brave. I wonder if spending two hours each morning looking into the mirror is making you feel better? If not, perhaps we could think together of ways to reduce this time. What sorts of things do you think might help you to do this? Are there things I could do to help you? I know it might be very tricky at first, but I am here to support you every step of the way. I have total confidence in your ability to give this a go.

Continue to validate your child, regardless of whether or not they are able to make steps away from or towards the mirror. While you may feel frustrated if progress is very slow (and your child is likely to feel very frustrated about this also), showing this frustration will make it less likely for your child to share openly with you in the future. Acknowledge that coming away from the mirror/looking into the mirror is very difficult for your child right now and offer them empathy and the opportunity to share their experiences without judgement, in order to alleviate any shame and fear they may be feeling.

We believe it is also important for you, as a parent, to consider your use of the mirror. If you are spending extended periods of time in front of the mirror yourself, are keeping magnified mirrors around the house and/or are making negative statements about yourself while gazing in the mirror, your child may find it more difficult to move beyond their difficult relationship with the looking glass. They may also find it more challenging to take up any suggestions you might make about their mirror use.

Camouflaging

Young people with BDD often go to great lengths to hide their perceived defect from others (and also, at times, from themselves).

This is often referred to as *camouflage*. These are some of the most common forms of camouflage your child may use:

- Clothing and accessories – jumpers, hats, scarves, glasses, etc.
- Make-up/cosmetics, particularly heavy layers of concealer/foundation.
- Hair, for example covering up parts of the face with the hair, having the hair cut in a particular way to conceal parts of the face, the shape of the head, etc.
- Plasters, bandages, etc.
- Piercings and tattoos (these are sometimes used to detract attention from the perceived defect).

Sadly, while young people tend to use camouflage to hide and therefore prevent attention being drawn to their perceived defect, they often actually end up drawing attention to themselves in the process. Wearing a hat and scarf in the summer weather, for example, is likely to provoke exactly the sort of stares and attention the young person is trying to avoid. This can lead to further feelings of shame and embarrassment and can reinforce the young person's belief that people are staring at them on account of the way they look.

It can be difficult for young people to 'give up' their make-up, extra clothing, etc. In many cases, using camouflage makes them feel more able to leave the house. It might be the difference between them feeling able to go to school and believing they cannot leave their bedroom at all. For these reasons, it is important to think very carefully and sensitively about any camouflage your child may be using. Prompting them to abruptly stop using their make-up completely, for example, may be 'too much too soon' and could lead to significant feelings of distress and a regression in terms of any progress that has been made. You might like to try:

- ☐ Being open and curious about your child's use of camouflage. This can include making curious rhetorical statements, for example, 'I have noticed you are wearing your cap around the house, Sam. I'm always here if that is something you feel like talking about.' It can also include asking open curious questions, for example, 'I have noticed you have been applying concealer before leaving your bedroom over the past few weeks, Sally. I am wondering why this might be.'
- ☐ Making open suppositions, while providing space for your child to tell you if you have 'got it wrong', for example, 'I could be wrong, Abdul, but I am wondering if wearing those plasters over your nose might be causing you to feel even more upset sometimes.'
- ☐ Refraining from becoming defensive if your child reacts defensively to your enquiries. Instead, acknowledge how difficult it is for your child to talk about this and remind them you are always here to talk, whenever they feel ready.
- ☐ Tentatively suggesting alternatives to the camouflage methods or intensities of camouflage your child is using, particularly if they are drawing greater attention to themselves, for example, 'You are telling me that you feel like people are staring at you, Jude. I wonder if it is because you are wearing so many clothes on such a

hot day. People are probably just curious as to why you have so many layers on in the heat, as most people are wearing short sleeves right now. Do you think this might have anything to do with why people may be looking at you? You have told me you want to cover up your arms. I understand this is causing you a lot of distress. I wonder if we could go shopping together to find some long-sleeved tops made of light material, or whether you would like to maybe try three-quarter length sleeves and see how this feels?'

☐ Maintaining your patience, regardless of how many times your child 'goes back' to their methods of camouflage. Commend them for their bravery regardless and continue to gently prompt them to make small changes, rather than expecting big changes to happen in short spaces of time.

Avoidance

Young people with BDD may feel embarrassed to go out in public with their perceived defect(s) on display. They often find it very difficult to imagine that other people do not see them as they see themselves; that other people do not see their 'defect', do not perceive them as 'ugly', nor are disgusted by them. Young people with BDD tend to expect rejection. They, therefore, typically avoid social interaction to negate experiences of possible rejection.

Sometimes, young people with BDD will think other people are staring at them or laughing at them. This is because the amygdala, the 'smoke detector' and 'fire alarm' part of the brain, tends to orientate towards that which is feared. The young person expects others to ridicule them and so this is what they believe they experience.

As we have already highlighted, young people with BDD are more likely to have been teased and bullied than young people without BDD. Teasing and bullying experiences can make young people more orientated towards potential threats in their environment, and towards potential rejection also. Exploring any teasing and bullying experiences with your child, with the support of education staff and therapeutic staff, is a very important element of addressing BDD. Some conversation starters for opening a discussion about potential bullying or teasing experiences are offered in the box below. There is some research to suggest that therapeutic approaches such as memory re-scripting, a type of therapy where the young person is invited back into the experience of the bullying event in order to 're-script' how they experienced and made sense of it, can be very beneficial when carried out by a trained professional.

Conversation starters for talking about bullying or teasing experiences

- You seem to have been coming home from school looking rather sad the last few weeks. Is there anything going on at school you would like to talk with me about?
- I have noticed your phone is going off a lot after school. Your friends seem to be in touch with you

very frequently. Do you like receiving these messages or are they tricky/upsetting sometimes? I was just wondering...

- There are always some unkind young people in every school/online, aren't there? Are any of these young people treating you unkindly at your school/online?
- It can be difficult to talk with people, particularly with parents, about being treated unkindly/being bullied/being teased at school, online or in other places. I wonder what would make it easier for you to talk to me if you were being teased? I would want to know if you were experiencing this. I feel I would be able to help.
- Sometimes young people are afraid to tell their parents they are being bullied because they think there is nothing their parents can do, or believe telling them might make things worse. I completely understand this. However, I also have the opinion that if parents listen openly to their children, and come up with strategies together, things can actually get better. What do you think?
- Have you come across the term, 'cyber-bullying'? I understand this is on the increase, particularly in young people and particularly through social media. Is this something you think it would be helpful for us to talk about? I am there for you if you are having any experiences like this. I would not intervene until we made an agreed plan of action together. (We will talk more about addressing cyber-bullying with your child in Chapter 9.)

Opening up conversations about past bullying or teasing experiences can be very important also, as these may have constituted 'triggering events' for your child's BDD.

It can be very frustrating, and extremely worrying, if your child is refusing to engage in social gatherings, to go to school or perhaps even to leave the house or their bedroom. Some young people with BDD become housebound; they refuse to leave the house at all for a period of time. Early intervention is important, wherever possible, to stop social avoidance behaviours from becoming entrenched. However, it is never too late to support your child to engage in the social aspects of life they used to enjoy.

There is a fine line between supporting your child to engage in social activities and 'pushing them' beyond that which they feel able to do. Drawing up a hierarchy, that is, drawing up a list of feared actions starting with the least threatening, as we will explore in more detail in Chapter 8, can be supportive to this end. This may begin with having family members over to the house all the way up to attending larger social gatherings like birthday parties and weddings.

For certain, it is important that your child does not become isolated while they are working their way up to feeling able to leave the bedroom, house or street. Some ideas to reduce social isolation include:

- ☐ Setting up Skype/Zoom-type video chats with single friends and groups of friends, even if the video screen is turned off in the early stages.
- ☐ Organising designated friends to bring missed schoolwork to them, to catch them up on school news, etc.
- ☐ Encouraging nurturing friends to visit often, even if just to pop around to say a quick 'hello'.

☐ Supporting your child to volunteer with groups by whom they are less likely to feel judged, for example, young children (volunteering in a nursery or special needs nursery), older people (volunteering in a residential home for older people) or animals (helping out in an animal shelter). Sometimes young people with BDD find the company of younger and older people much less threatening than the company of people of their own age. They can also often find the company of animals very relieving and soothing, as they feel the animal is not noticing or focused on their perceived defect(s) the way they believe humans might be.

☐ Keeping family meals 'light' in terms of conversation, and considering making amendments to these meals in order to make them feel less 'threatening' for your child, for example, keeping the curtains closed or removing mirrors from the room.

☐ Continuing to talk to your child regularly, even if they are isolating themselves in their bedroom. Set aside regular times to come into their bedroom (or sit outside their door) chatting to them about light-hearted topics. There can sometimes be a propensity for parents to want to engage in heavy, problem-solving talk with their child when they see that they are struggling, but often what young people need most at these times is the opportunity to simply connect and relate. Deeper topics can always be explored later, when your child is feeling more settled. Use of Bruce Perry's model of relating can be supportive (see the box on the following page).

☐ Continuing to offer and provide (with consent) touch

of some developmentally appropriate form, for example, your hand over their hand, hugs, foot rubs or shoulder massages (both offered by you and received by you from the young person).

☐ Refraining from losing sight of what your child typically enjoys or is passionate about. Often, hobbies, passions and even personality traits (such as a sense of humour) can get 'lost' under all the BDD-related compulsions and preoccupations. Keep the flame of your child's personality, passions and interests alive by continually inviting them back into the activities they used to enjoy, even if just for a few minutes each day.

Bruce Perry's Three-Step Model for Relational Connection

- *Regulate* – use the tone of your voice, your posture, etc. to support your child to regulate their fight/flight/freeze/fawn[1] responses and to help them come to a place of calm and safety within.
- *Relate* – connect with your child through empathy, compassion and touch to help them to feel heard and validated.
- *Reason* – reflect together with your child on how they are feeling and consider ways forward together. (Perry, 2010, 2013; Perry and Hambrick, 2008)

---

1   To fawn is to lay aside one's needs significantly for another person's needs, to submit to another's will without any thought for one's personal needs and desires.

Reassurance seeking

Young people with BDD often believe the way they see themselves is the way others see them. They often think if people say 'nice things' about them, particularly about their appearance, they are just trying to make them feel better, and are lying to them. Young people with BDD often spend a lot of time trying to glean as accurate as possible an understanding of what other people think they look like. In order to do this, they typically engage in lots of reassurance seeking: asking other people how they think they look, whether they can see their perceived appearance defect and so on.

Engaging in reassurance-seeking cycles with your child is very unlikely to be fruitful. In truth, your child is very unlikely, for the reasons already described, to believe what you tell them anyway. If moving beyond BDD was as simple as reassuring your child they do not have an appearance defect, specialized therapies and books like this would not be necessary.

Rather than responding directly to reassurance seeking by telling your child that they look fine to you, you cannot see their blemishes, are always beautiful in your eyes, etc., it can be more helpful to gently move away from getting drawn into a circular debate about who is right and who isn't. We recommend that you try not to engage in conversations about appearance, especially about specific aspects of the appearance. We find it is generally more beneficial to focus on the distress your child is feeling, and on any resultant impairment in their ability to engage with and enjoy life as they typically would. In our experience, getting drawn into giving reassurance can cause further distress or conflict and tends, at best, to only offer very short-term relief.

It can really help to acknowledge the deeper drive underlying your child's reassurance seeking: the drive to feel soothed and validated. Some of the following responses may be helpful:

- ☐ It sounds like you are feeling a bit scared/insecure/shaky right now. I am so sorry you are feeling this way. Can I give you a hug?
- ☐ I don't think you will believe me if I tell you that your skin looks fine to me. So I wonder if we can talk about your underlying feelings of fear/anxiety instead.

Appearance-related comparisons

Comparing one's appearance to the appearance of others, particularly comparing the appearance of a particular body part to the same body part of others, is a very common experience for young people with BDD. This can be both exhausting and distressing. This behaviour can link very closely to the reassurance-seeking behaviours we have just explored.

Young people might compare aspects of their appearance to people in their family, friends, media figures or strangers. They might spend hours on the internet comparing their appearance to celebrities. They may also take 'selfies' of themselves in order to compare how their skin, for example, changes from one day, or even one hour or minute, to the next. Some young people also use various electronic apps to assess and track their appearance. We will explore this in more detail in Chapter 9.

Naturally, it is important that parents/family members, etc. do not compare the appearance of their child to that of other people in any way, for example, siblings, cousins or peers. If you have done this in the past, and are now feeling guilty about it, please bear in mind that BDD is never caused by a single event, experience or person. BDD is far more complex than this. It is never too late to change our narratives and relate to our children and their appearance in new ways.

Your child is likely to be comparing their appearance/body part to that of others in order to both gain an accurate internal image of their own appearance/body part and to glean a clear visual sense of how they would like their appearance/body part to look. Typically, making repeated appearance-related comparisons leads to feelings of inadequacy and shame. If you notice your child engaging in such comparisons, you may like to support them in the following ways:

- ☐ Gently guiding them away from spending too much time on the internet, social media or looking at magazines.
- ☐ Encouraging them to un-follow unhealthy influences on social media, and to find more positive role models online.
- ☐ Noticing when they are staring at others an non-judgementally acknowledging this, for example, 'Are you okay, Gurmanaat? You seem to be looking over at that lady quite a bit and seem rather anxious. Shall we have a chat about that nature programme we saw yesterday to take your mind off it?'.
- ☐ Noticing when they are staring at others and gently re-directing their attention, for example, by offering to play a game with them (e.g. name an animal beginning with each letter of the alphabet, or the 'I went to the shops and I bought...' memory game), or providing a hobby

that occupies the eyes (e.g. bringing sewing or drawing materials along when you go on public transport).

☐ Refraining, yourself, from engaging in comparisons in front of your child, for example, comparing yourself to your friends or colleagues. It can be very easy to do this, and it can seem very harmless, but something as simple as stating that you wish you had hair like your friend's hair, for example, gives a strong message to your child and can be a trigger-point for their BDD.

Attempts to fix the perceived defect including the seeking of cosmetic surgery, dentistry, dermatology or use of over-the-counter products

Seeking methods of 'fixing' the perceived defect is often a key aspect of the experience of BDD. Young people may seek cosmetic surgery, dentistry and dermatological treatments or procedures, etc. in order to 'fix' the aspects of their appearance they believe are defective or flawed. They may also try 'do-it-yourself' procedures at home or seek out products, like skin-care products, to 'fix' their perceived defect. Some of the do-it-yourself procedures young people have told us about include putting weights on their stomach to flatten it; pushing their teeth into the bedframe to realign them; pushing their nose into wooden surfaces to alter its shape; and using strong, abrasive skin products to remove the top layer of their skin. Some of the treatments young people might seek can include dental work, lipo-suction, cosmetic surgery, Botox injections, dermatological treatments like antibiotics and topical treatments, and hair-loss reversal medication.

Research very clearly demonstrates that cosmetic and other physical procedures very rarely have beneficial outcomes for people with BDD. More often than not, the person will feel dissatisfied with the outcome of the treatment, either going on to seek further treatments or attempting to 'fix' things via do-it-yourself procedures at home. Even if the young person feels the outcome of their treatment or surgery is successful, it is highly possible the focus of their appearance-attention will move on to another body part, as their core sense of unworthiness and feelings of anxiety are still there.

It is understandable that many parents of children with BDD take their child along to dermatological, dentistry or cosmetic surgery appointments. Their child may have told them if they could just have their perceived defect fixed, their distress would reduce. Parents are generally desperate to help their child to feel better about themselves. As a result, they may concede to taking them along to, and paying for, such appointments and treatments. However, when parents agree to such treatments young people typically take this to be confirmation that there is an appearance defect present. If the dermatologist, dentist or cosmetic surgeon then agrees to provide a treatment or procedure, the young person may feel they have further 'proof' that an actual defect is there and is serious enough to warrant intervention. As we have described, we also know from the research that young people are typically dissatisfied with the outcomes of any cosmetic appointment or procedures they undergo. As one young person explained to us:

'My mum wants to be there and to be helpful and so she booked me really expensive dermatology appointments and stuff but none of it really worked.'

It can be very difficult to refrain from supporting your child in seeking out and obtaining physical treatments, or from buying skin-care products or teeth-whitening products, etc. for them when they ask. It can be the source of much conflict in families and can even lead to aggressive outbursts in some cases. Your child may even tell you that if they don't receive the surgery or skin-care products they feel they will hurt themselves or try to end their lives. As a parent, this is one of the most terrifying things you can hear. We will look at suicidality in BDD in detail together in Chapter 5.

In treatment for BDD, clinicians focus on the distress caused by the BDD and the impact this is having on the young person's (and, indeed, other family members') lives. As part of this, treatment for BDD includes reducing the preoccupation with cosmetic surgery, dentistry, dermatology, etc. and on letting go of the need to compulsively buy (or ask parents to buy) skin-care products or similar. We recommend that parents acknowledge their child's desire to try out yet another facewash, for example, while gently explaining why buying such a product would not be in the young person's best interests. You might like to remind your child that buying them facewashes in the past has not reduced their level of distress and that you believe that money would be better spent on buying your child something to enhance their wellbeing such as a craft kit or a new book about their favourite hobby. This may ignite frustration and disappointment in your child, as they may believe you are withholding what they believe they require in order to feel better about themselves or are punishing them in some way. Acknowledge this disappointment while gently reminding your child that you love them and only have their best interests at heart.

If your child is pinning all their hope of feeling better onto possible surgery etc., the last thing we want to do is to completely take this hope away. It tends to work better to ask your child to suspend their plans for physical treatments for the time being, while acknowledging how difficult this is and how much courage it demands. With the right psychological treatment, we know that young people often stop wishing for cosmetic treatments and appearance-focused products and are pleased they never underwent the procedures they had previously been hoping for.

A note about skin picking

When the focus of attention is on the young person's skin, skin picking can be very common. Your child may be spending long stretches of time picking at their skin, in front of or away from the mirror, in an attempt to remove perceived blemishes and to smoothen the skin. In reality, skin picking can fuel a vicious circle whereby picking at the skin causes physical blemishes and scars which, in turn, increases their use of make-up and levels of distress. Seeking professional support for your child to terminate this cycle is vital both for their immediate wellbeing and to prevent long-term scarring and damage to their skin.

Compulsive skin picking can be a very difficult thing to overcome and often requires professional help. Do make any involved professionals aware if your child is regularly picking at their skin and support your child with any suggested actions, such as keeping their hands busy with other things (e.g. fiddling with Tangles or a piece of Blu Tack, threading beads, creating artwork, knitting, squeezing a soft ball); wearing cotton gloves; setting a timer for their time in front of the mirror or in the bathroom; increasing the time between the urge to pick and touching the skin (e.g. by counting or using a timer on the phone or similar); engaging in other self-soothing sensory experiences like chewing menthol gum or smelling lavender on a handkerchief; and engaging in other 'picking' activities like picking paint off a wooden pencil, unpicking threads and pulling weeds. It will also be helpful to encourage your child to keep their nails trimmed and to keep any wounds clean to avoid infection. Removing all tweezers and pins from the house may also be beneficial.

CHAPTER 3

The Impact of BDD on the Family

BDD can have a far-reaching and profound impact on the family. This chapter will explore the impact having a child with BDD can have on family members, relationships, family functioning and life in general. We hope this will help you to feel that you are not alone in your experience. We will discuss the common issues parents face, including how you may feel about having a child with BDD; disagreement regarding the BDD diagnosis; how families often accommodate BDD in an attempt to help their child; and the impact of BDD on the family more generally, including on sibling relationships.

How you may feel about having a child with BDD

Parents and carers often do not realize their child has BDD until it starts to have a significant impact on the child's functioning, for example, their child begins to struggle to get to school in the morning and to show high levels of distress. As you read in Chapter 1, the diagnostic criteria for BDD highlights a significant impact on functioning. Indeed, experiences of distress are hallmarks of BDD.

Sometimes, parents tell us that they feel guilty about not having noticed the signs of BDD sooner and intervened earlier. However, we ask you to hold in mind that noticing BDD in the early stages tends to be really difficult. BDD is often hidden from others due to the high levels of shame and embarrassment young people experience related to their concerns. Your child may have felt that if they talked to you or others about their appearance-related distress, they would have come across as vain or conceited. It is also common for people to think the appearance distress and related behaviours are all part of being a teenager, and you may have thought the same. Alternatively, your child may have spoken to you about their appearance preoccupations but this may have led to conflict or disagreement. Your child may have been trying to convince you that there is a flaw in their appearance that you simply cannot see; this is another hallmark of the condition. Please feel assured, all of this is extremely common. It is not your fault that you did not notice the symptoms earlier. As one young person explained to us:

'Neither myself nor my family had ever heard of BDD. We didn't know what it was and couldn't even really place my feelings as being about appearance necessarily. Looking back now I can see I was doing things like checking the mirrors at school, scanning the area and sort of listening to what other kids were saying. I would assume they were talking about me or that if they laughed, they were laughing at me. But we kind of just assumed it was normal behaviour, I guess. It just become so natural that I didn't even instinctively think it was a behaviour of the BDD. It wasn't until I stopped going to school that we realized there was probably a bigger issue at play.'

Many parents can sometimes feel guilty for other reasons. For example, some parents tell us that they feel guilty that they cannot reduce their child's distress in day-to-day life. As a parent, you may see it as part of your role to regulate and soothe your child when they are upset, yet you may now find that you are in a situation where this may not feel possible all, or even some of, the time. It may be that you don't have a sense of what to do to help your child to feel better. Some parents tell us they feel guilty about needing to get on with other things in life, such as going to work, or looking after other children or family members. It may be that you are not able to focus solely on your child who has BDD. All in all, guilt appears to be a very common feeling for many parents of children with BDD.

Another common feeling parents often describe, which is related to guilt, is that they feel they are to blame in some way. Parents sometimes tell us they feel they could have done something to stop their child from developing BDD. Often parents talk about their child's early development and say, 'If I had done this differently, maybe my child would not have ended up with BDD.' We would like to reiterate that it is nobody's fault that your child developed BDD.

Grief or a sense of loss is sometimes described by parents of young people with BDD. They talk about how their child has become consumed by BDD and behaves in ways that are not in keeping with the child they were before. Parents may miss the child they had prior to suffering with BDD. You may feel at times that you have completely lost your child to BDD, which can be incredibly upsetting. These are very common feelings and reactions, yet it is important to hold in mind that there is always hope, and that there are treatments available that will give your child back to you, and them back to themselves (see Chapters 7 and 8 for more information about treatment for BDD). We know the journey to getting the right treatment, and the journey through treatment, can feel long and you may feel there is not an end in sight at times. Please know that many parents whose children have now found ways to cope with, and even completely move beyond, their BDD once felt this way also.

One mother shared this insight with us:

> 'My advice is don't blame yourself for any of this. Be there for the BDD sufferer and try and spend a lot of time with them. Make sure they know you are there for them. Remember when their awful behaviours are out of character it is not them, it is their BDD demon. Don't take the aggression personally; this is very hard and you will feel hurt, frustrated and angry at times. Remember your child will come back after recovery and return to their lovely personality again.'

Many other emotions can emerge related to having a child with BDD. These emotions may not just be related to the diagnosis of BDD, but also to the impact BDD has on family life and relationships. Parents are often exhausted, anxious, stressed, hopeless and/or depressed on account of their child's BDD. This can then have an impact on other aspects of life, possibly including relationships with a partner and other family members, work, social life, etc. In the next section we will discuss the various ways BDD can impact on, and manifest in, family life, which will, we hope, help you to see that it is completely understandable that family life can be disrupted, and your own mental health affected.

It is important to highlight here that you may need to seek some individual support for yourself. Please do not forget yourself, including your own emotional and psychological needs, in all of this. In order to be able to cope with the situation and to support your child, you need to make sure that you are well too. We often remind parents that on a plane you are always told to put your own oxygen mask on before you help others. The same applies to supporting your child with BDD (see Chapter 10 for ideas related to your own self-care).

Disagreement regarding BDD diagnosis

A source of tension and conflict in the family is likely to be due to the fact your child may not think a BDD diagnosis fits with their experience as you do. They may see it as an issue with their physical appearance, as opposed to an emotional and psychological problem. This fundamental difference in opinion may lead to arguments and conflict in the family. It may be extremely frustrating and upsetting for you to know that your child is utterly convinced they have flaws or defects in their appearance, despite the fact that you and others do not see them. It can be very difficult not to get caught up in unhelpful conversations, wherein you are trying to convince your child they look fine or that you cannot see what they see. As you may know from your own experience, these conversations are unlikely to help your child to feel any better or to convince them there isn't a flaw or defect in their appearance.

It may be stressful for the whole family in terms of what you collectively consider to be the solution to the problem. Your child may be badgering you for surgery, products, cosmetic interventions, new clothes, etc. and this can put pressure on you to respond to these requests. This may have financial implications and also be a source of tension and arguments, as you may have a sense that these pursuits are unlikely to reduce your child's distress in the long term. You may have provided your child with what they have asked for in terms of physical treatments, cosmetic products or clothing and discovered this only gives them short-term relief and does not solve the issue or diminish their anxiety in the long term. There may be differing views between family members about how to manage these conversations and requests. This, again, may cause tension between you and your child, and perhaps also between you and other family members.

Although disagreement about the diagnosis is common in the early stages, we have also worked with many young people who eventually came around not only to accepting the diagnosis of BDD but also experiencing a sense of relief from this diagnosis. Therefore, we recommend you hold on to hope and continue to gently have open conversations with your child about the nature of their difficulties. Continue to suggest that the issue they are struggling with may be psychological and not physical in nature, all the while focusing on the impact the issue is having on their daily life. One young person, who had previously very much believed she had real defects in her appearance and had been seeking cosmetic treatments shared with us:

'The consultant sent a letter saying, "You have BDD; this is the NHS's definition, and this is some recommended reading." My family came to visit me – they read the letter and were like, "Oh my goodness, this is you." It was like this validation. It explained so much. There was this sense of relief because, upon reflection, those years between the ages of eight and eighteen were so turbulent for me and my family. I love them so much and to put them through the stuff I did... I know it wasn't my fault but now I had a reason, a bit of a rationale, as to why I behaved the way I did. I felt like it was just something we all needed. So the diagnosis of BDD was definitely a relief in that sense.'

Family accommodation of BDD (the things you may do to relieve your child's BDD)

'Family accommodation' is a term used to describe how family members alter their behaviour to alleviate the distress of a relative suffering with a mental health condition. Parents have described a range of ways they have accommodated BDD, which itself can have an impact on family members. For example, parents often describe having to get directly involved with BDD-related repetitive behaviours and rituals: helping their child with their grooming rituals; responding to requests to check their child's appearance; or providing their child with the funds for products, such as skin-care products, or procedures such as dental surgery. Funding products and procedures can put a financial strain on the family. This can particularly be the case if your child takes to buying a range of products and stops using them after a short time in the pursuit of another product or procedure, as they do not 'fix' the perceived flaw or defect as they hoped they would.

Often, young people with BDD seek reassurance, asking for confirmation that others can see the flaw or that they really are as ugly as they think they are. This can cause a huge amount of conflict and have a negative impact on family relationships, particularly as you will not be able to see the defect as your child perceives it. You may have noticed that these reassurance-seeking conversations can get rather heated. You may find yourself trying to convince your child they look okay, while they are trying to convince you there is a problem with their physical appearance. Your child may feel as though you are not taking their concerns seriously or are dismissing them, when actually you simply don't see what they see, in the way they see it. We will come back to some ideas about how to talk to your child about BDD in Chapter 4. As one young person described it:

> 'People would tell me, "Oh, you know, you look fine. What's your issue? You're an attractive young girl. What's your problem?" But I didn't see that. I thought they were lying to me and just trying to trick me.'

Your child may avoid certain situations, particularly social situations, because of BDD. We know that at least a third of the young people seen in specialist BDD services are housebound (not able to leave the house) and/or are not consistently attending school. Some young people with BDD struggle to be seen even by their parents or other members of the family, which can be incredibly heart-breaking for the whole family. You might find yourself facilitating your child's avoidance. For example, some parents say they have taken down or covered up mirrors around their home because their child becomes extremely distressed by seeing their reflection, or gets stuck in front of the mirror checking their perceived flaw or defect. Other parents have described driving their child everywhere or paying for taxis as their child is so anxious about using public transport and being seen by others. Some families have told us they take meals to their child in their bedroom as they struggle to sit and eat downstairs with the rest of the family. One young person explained to us:

> 'I'd go months without going outside. I'd be in the lounge and I couldn't even sit in my own living room with the curtains open because I was afraid that someone would see me with no make-up on and that freaked me out.'

You may have had to change your work patterns to fit in with your child's BDD. For example, you may have had to start going into work later if your child struggles with getting ready in the morning or spends hours getting dressed, applying make-up or checking themselves in the mirror. Some parents have given up work altogether because they are concerned about leaving their child unsupervised (see Chapter 5 on responding to hopelessness and suicidality). This can put a huge financial pressure on the family, especially if coupled with spending money on products and procedures in a bid to help your child feel better about their appearance.

There are a magnitude of ways families accommodate BDD in

order to reduce the distress their child is experiencing. However, we know this distress reduction is typically temporary. You may find you end up doing more and more to accommodate your child's BDD – this can become a vicious cycle. We know family accommodation reinforces BDD and keeps the emphasis on appearance and on the need to fix/hide perceived flaws. We also know how difficult it can be to refrain from accommodation and that there may be times when accommodating your child's BDD is the safest and most appropriate course of action.

Sometimes, young people tell us they have a positive view of family accommodation; they may perceive it as reducing their appearance concern in the short term. They may also take it to be an indication that you, as their parent, perceive there to be a problem with their appearance, as why (to their mind) would you buy them dermatological products, for example, if you didn't also believe their skin was blemished? You may feel really torn between accommodating and not accommodating your child's BDD, particularly as your natural instinct is likely to be to attempt to bring your child's distress down.

It can be very difficult to know what to do instead of accommodating BDD. Indeed, in many instances, families may need to accommodate the BDD until they are receiving appropriate therapeutic support. A clear treatment plan can really help (see Chapter 8). It can be perplexing to know what to do without a plan developed in collaboration with your child, as the consequences of not accommodating may be difficult to manage in the family without guidance and support. Here are some pointers in terms of what you might like to try.

Advice for speaking to your child about family accommodation

☐ Arrange a time to speak to your child about the accommodation you have noticed and give them a chance to prepare for that discussion.

☐ In a neutral and non-judgemental tone, ask your child if they have noticed any changes in how they are feeling, in what they may be doing and how the family dynamic is operating.

☐ Get alongside your child and share the dilemma and concerns, for example, 'We seem to agree that things are difficult in the family at the moment. I wonder if we can think of some changes we can make together to make things feel a bit better for everyone?'

☐ Examples of the steps to challenge BDD-related accommodation will be different for everyone, but may include setting time limits/scheduling times for bathroom use, uncovering mirrors for set times of the day so other family members can use them, agreeing on limits regarding how much to spend on products or agreeing how to respond to your child when they ask for reassurance.

☐ It is important to acknowledge this is a stressful time for your child. Explain that you can keep discussing and breaking down the steps if the first trial of challenging/reducing elements of family accommodation proves to be too difficult.

☐ It is helpful to share with your child that while any steps towards reducing family accommodation may feel challenging at first, it will get easier. Remind your child regularly of the rationale for your actions, for example, 'We have been covering mirrors for a while and we know everyone needs to use the mirrors, so it is important for family life that we try to compromise.'

☐ It may be useful to highlight to your child that, despite family accommodation, they are still distressed, and their appearance worries are still impacting on their day-to-day life. Therefore, the accommodation is not making things better in the long run. Suggest that perhaps support outside of the family may be needed, for example, seeing a therapist who specializes in supporting young people with BDD.

Impact of BDD on family relationships

Family relationships are likely to be strained because of BDD for a range of reasons. Anyone can be affected and there is normally an impact on siblings. If you have more than one child, it can be challenging as a parent to balance the needs of your other children. Siblings can feel neglected or overlooked and may feel their sibling with BDD is getting preferential treatment, particularly if they do not understand what is driving their sibling's distress. They, too, may have to accommodate their sibling's BDD, which can put a huge pressure on them.

Parents often tell us that there is tension between their children. Sometimes they describe how their child(ren) without BDD makes negative comments about their sibling's appearance when arguing. This can be difficult to manage as a parent and there is no right or wrong way of doing this. You may wish to consider whether your other child(ren) needs their own emotional or psychological support. Here are some ideas for supporting other family members affected by BDD:

Supporting family members affected by BDD

☐ Set some time aside to speak to your other child(ren) and/or family members to find out how they are feeling and what impact the BDD may be having on their lives. Remember they are likely to be feeling similar emotions to yourself.

☐ Think together about what they feel they may need so they feel supported. Consider together some ideas about how they can manage things, for example, one-to-one time with you doing something they enjoy, more time to discuss how they are feeling, reduction of their involvement in the BDD.

☐ It can be helpful to remind your other child(ren) that it is not their sibling's (with BDD) fault they are behaving this way; they are not behaving in this way to purposefully hurt family members but because they are struggling with a mental health condition.

☐ Encourage your other children to share things they continue to enjoy in relation to their relationship with their sibling, for example spending time playing board games together.

You may find that BDD can also lead to challenges with the extended family (e.g. aunts, uncles and grandparents), friends and others who know the young person. There may be differences in opinion about how the behaviours related to BDD should be managed. Sometimes parents share with us that they feel criticized by others, for example, grandparents saying that the young person with BDD needs more discipline. This can be very difficult. It may be helpful for you to share with others what BDD is and how it is impacting on family life, to increase their insight into the condition. It may be helpful to discuss with family members and friends what would happen if you followed their advice, for example, that if you stopped your child from using camouflage overnight your child would become extremely distressed.

It is important for others to understand what you are going through. By sharing your experience and knowledge of BDD, including by directing others towards information and resources (such as the BDD Foundation website) it can increase understanding and provide a potential source of support for you and your child. Remember, you are doing the best you can in very difficult circumstances. For more guidance on speaking to, and enlisting the support of, family members please see Chapter 10.

You may feel you no longer recognize your child

Parents often describe feeling like they have lost their child to BDD. BDD is extremely distressing for the sufferer which may make them behave in ways that are not in keeping with their personality and temperament. As one young person explained to us:

'I think, I have always considered that I almost have two minds in my head. One is the BDD and one is who I actually am.'

Many young people exhibit their distress in the form of aggression, which may be verbal but can also be physical in nature. Parents tell us this can be very difficult to manage at home. While distress-related outbursts are an understandable response to the experience of BDD, it is also important to hold your family values in mind, including what is typically deemed in your family to be acceptable and unacceptable. This should help you to judge how to respond to displays of aggression (we will discuss this in more detail in the next chapter).

It is important to remember that, even when your child is behaving in ways that feel unrecognizable to you, your child's core self is still there and will come back to the foreground when they have learned to manage, and/or moved beyond, their BDD. Many parents tell us, with great delight, about how their child's interests, hobbies and personality re-emerged after treatment. We will help you to think further about how to maintain hope and plans for a future after BDD in Chapter 12. We find these words of one young person who spent many years struggling with BDD very hopeful:

'As I've developed and had therapy and met different people and had different experiences, I've been able to evolve into who I truly am. Freedom! I was held captive in certain negative thoughts and was freed from them. I feel the image of a butterfly emerging from a cocoon is the example of my journey with BDD. I now feel I'm really quite free from body dysmorphia.'

CHAPTER 4

Managing the Impact of BDD on the Family

We looked at the range of ways BDD can impact on family life in Chapter 3. This chapter sets out some ideas about how to manage this impact. It is important to highlight here that these are general guidelines to help you to manage. However, the best outcomes are likely to happen if the advice you are given is specifically tailored to your child by a mental health professional who specializes in BDD – one size certainly does not fit all with BDD, or indeed with any mental health condition. We have included this chapter as we know you may have not accessed mental health support yet. It will be important to do so and there is some advice on how to go about this in Chapter 7. We suggest the stage before your child begins treatment should be focused on trying to keep things as stable as possible.

How to talk to your child about BDD

There are all sorts of stages regarding having conversations with your child about BDD. You may not have broached the topic with your child at all yet, or you may be further down the line and have mentioned BDD to your child. Or maybe BDD has been mentioned to your child by somebody else, such as another family member or peer. Ultimately, there is likely to be fundamental disagreement about the diagnosis of BDD. Your child may believe the issue is related to their physical appearance while you may conceptualize the issue as being emotional and psychological in nature.

While diagnoses are important for accessing the right support, it may be less important to discuss the specific diagnosis of BDD with your child. It is likely that if you focus too much on the diagnosis of BDD, your child's anxiety may increase and they could find it difficult to engage in a helpful conversation about their struggles. It may be important, instead, to focus on the elements of the diagnosis that you and your child are likely to agree on: that is, on the distress and impairment the various worries and behaviours are causing. Often therapists use this focus on distress and impairment as a way to engage young people in treatment. This approach often proves to be fruitful as parent and child can typically agree that the worries are causing distress and impairment in activities of daily living. It is these elements the treatment focuses on reducing.

We hope it is becoming clear that we think it is important to resist getting into an argument with your child about whether they have BDD or not. We also believe it can be unhelpful to engage in conversations about whether or not there is a flaw or defect in your child's appearance. This may be very tricky, and you may have to watch out for these reassurance-seeking conversations, especially in heated moments. We suggest getting alongside your child and perhaps saying something like,

'I know your appearance worries are making you distressed' or, 'It is difficult to say what I see or don't see as I know our views on reality differ. However, I can see this is stressing you out and I want to help.' It is important to acknowledge that these kinds of reflections may not reduce your child's distress in the short term. Your child may continue to badger you for an answer or reassurance. It is, therefore, important for you to acknowledge their distress consistently so they feel heard.

If you are finding it increasingly difficult not to get pulled into conversations with your child about the specific aspects of their appearance they are worried about, you could perhaps share your dilemma with them in an age-appropriate way. You could tell them you are finding it difficult to know how to respond to them when you each have such different views about what is going on. Remember, again, to highlight that you know how stressful this is for them, and do not be afraid to let them know that it is stressful for you also. If the diagnosis of BDD has been raised by you or others – and you are, therefore, further down the line with the conversation – it may still be important to follow this advice regarding how to manage these discussions. Below are some reminders about how to have conversations about BDD with your child:

Having conversations about BDD with your child

☐ Do not focus on the label of BDD too much but rather focus on the impact and distress the appearance concerns are causing.

☐ Explain to your child that you know this is not about vanity. Validate that they are experiencing genuine distress and preoccupations.

☐ Do not minimize what your child is experiencing nor advise them to try to accept or cope with their perceived flaw; comments like, 'You just need to accept your skin the way it is' may be very unhelpful and distressing for your child.

☐ Although difficult, try to avoid getting into conversations about the specific perceived flaw. Avoid discussing whether or not you see what your child sees as this can cause tension and conflict. It can be helpful to acknowledge that this perceived flaw is their experience and that you recognize the impact this perception is having on their life.

☐ You may decide a conversation is too difficult at certain points. You can, instead, invite your child to access some resources and information about BDD, such as those on the BDD Foundation website, to help them build insight into their concerns and difficulties. We also recommend sharing with your child the book *Appearance Anxiety* (2019) by the clinicians at the National and Specialist OCD, BDD and Related Disorders Clinic at the Maudsley Hospital in London.

Many parents have found it can be helpful to open up conversations about BDD at calm times and to avoid the times when their child is in the midst of their BDD distress or engaging in

BDD-related behaviours. Your child is likely, on some level, to find the conversation threatening anyway, so having this conversation when their threat system is in full force may lead to an escalation of their distress. Find a calm time to speak to your child and share with them what you have noticed in terms of the distress they are experiencing and any associated behaviours you have seen. This may then lead to a conversation about what help may be needed in order to manage the distress and the impact this is having, rather than attempting to manage their distress by attempting to 'fix' their perceived defect or flaw. Your child may respond to the conversation by suggesting a solution to change something about their physical appearance. This is an invitation for you to flag up that there may be other options to explore outside of physical treatments and products.

These sorts of conversations are typically needed more than once. You may have to keep having these conversations until your child is willing to consider mental health support. While these conversations alone may not lead to your child's agreement to seek psychological services, it is important to be consistent and to keep having them regardless. We know it can feel very anxiety-provoking for parents to have these conversations as they often feel unsure about how their child will respond. It can also be difficult to find the time alongside everything you have going on to have these conversations, but their importance cannot be over-estimated. These kinds of discussions may support your child to acknowledge what is going on and to build insight into their difficulties. They may also potentially increase your child's receptivity to seeking and receiving help. One young person told us that it really helped her to have open conversations with her mum during her struggle with BDD:

'I got closer with my mum and my family which helped me. It meant my mum didn't always have to feel like she needed to ask me how I was doing or give me all those books on BDD because we could just talk more openly about it.'

How to manage family accommodation

As we explored in Chapter 3, you may be doing an array of things as a family to accommodate your child's BDD. As you may recall, family accommodation refers to how you and other family members may be altering your behaviour to alleviate distress for your child with BDD. It is difficult to advise on what to do or not do in relation to family accommodation before BDD treatment begins, as this is typically best done in the context of treatment. However, our aim is to offer some general advice in this chapter as a starting point or to supplement targeted therapeutic advice and support.

It is important to try to keep things as stable as possible before treatment begins. It may be helpful for you and other family members to monitor what you are having to do for your child to accommodate the BDD, as this can be helpful to discuss with professionals. You might like to keep a simple diary or journal, for example writing down the small and big things you do each day to accommodate your child's BDD. The likelihood is you will have got pulled into accommodating in various ways. At this stage, therefore, it may be about continuing what you are doing while being aware that this is reinforcing the BDD and being careful not to start engaging in new accommodating behaviours.

It may be helpful, in a calm moment, to discuss with your child what you have noticed in terms of what you are doing to accommodate their concerns. You can reflect that while it is completely understandable that they feel they need you to do certain things, or for certain things to be altered in the family home and routine, it does not seem to be helping them as they are continuing to be distressed. These kinds of conversations may serve two functions. They may help your child to build insight into their difficulties as they may not have realized how much family accommodation was taking place; and they may provide you with a foundation to suggest that accommodating BDD further is unhelpful. Let your child know that your suggestion of not accommodating the BDD in new ways comes from a place of caring about them and, as their parent, part of your role is to make decisions you believe are in their best interests.

If your child is in agreement, it may be helpful to set out with them what you are willing to do and not do in terms of accommodation. It will be important to be clear that you will do your utmost to stick with these agreed boundaries. It may be helpful to write down what has been agreed so there is concrete evidence that can be referred to in more difficult moments, such as when your child may be requesting things. If your child seems to be requesting more and more of something, such as increasing amounts of reassurance, this could also be sensitively highlighted to them. This may help your child to see that they would benefit from finding other ways to manage their distress.

When you are trying to set boundaries around family accommodation, you may feel anxious and torn about what to do. On the one hand, you may feel compelled to do something to alleviate your child's distress in the moment but, on the other hand, you may have a sense that this may maintain their difficulties and distress in the long term. It will be important that the boundaries you set are in line with what you feel you can manage and are able to adhere to. There will also need to be an agreement with other family members involved to do the same. Inconsistency in managing BDD can make your child even more anxious and perpetuate their difficulties. We absolutely acknowledge that this process can be just as difficult for you as it is for your child.

Below is a summary of some ideas on how to manage family accommodation.

Tips for managing family accommodation

☐ Gently share some of your observations of accommodating behaviour with your child in a neutral and non-judgemental tone, for example, 'I have noticed you have been asking us for more and more skin products and we keep buying them for you. I wonder if our actions are actually helping you or if they may be making things worse.'

☐ Share how difficult it can feel for you to know what to do for the best, for example, 'I know you are really finding it difficult to come and have dinner with us and it is really distressing for you. It is sad for us too that we do not get to spend as much time with you. I am not sure what to do for the best as we want you with us for meals, but we know how difficult it is for you.'

☐ Try to think with your child about some of the ways you can reduce some of the accommodating behaviours, for example, 'I know this is challenging, but I wonder whether we can think together of ways to try and face some of these difficult situations. For example, maybe we can try to limit how much money is spent on your face creams, so you can challenge yourself and it will help the family to save some money.'

It is best to have these conversations in calmer moments when your child is not anxious or distressed.

How to manage aggression

As we discussed in Chapter 3, young people with BDD experience high levels of distress which can at times result in challenging behaviour. This might include verbal aggression, threats to harm themselves and lashing out. It is important to hold in mind that while this is very much due to your child's BDD, you would do well to adhere to boundaries within your family related to what is acceptable and unacceptable behaviour. You can manage BDD-related aggression or other behaviours that are unacceptable in your family in the same way you would do for a child without BDD. This may be additionally difficult given your child is suffering from BDD and there is a clear reason for the behaviour. However, if consequences are not put in place, these behaviours may continue to occur or even escalate. This is no small task; your child's distress may rise as you attempt to deal with aggressive behaviour, and you may be fearful of increasing risk (see Chapter 5 for ideas about how to manage risk). You may feel more confident in confronting your child's aggression if they are engaging with mental health services, so you have support in place should any risk-related issues arise.

If you choose to implement consequences for aggression, it will be important that you explain clearly that the behaviour exhibited is not acceptable. Whilst doing so, it is important to be sensitive to feelings of shame that may be triggered by this process. We very much recommend separating BDD behaviours from the young person, which means emphasizing that it is the behaviour you are feeling upset by and are unhappy with, not your child themselves. Explain that while you understand the behaviours are coming from a place of distress due to appearance concerns (and that you know your child's intention isn't to be aggressive) there are still boundaries that need to be respected within your family. This approach can be helpful if your child has siblings, who may believe your child with BDD is receiving preferential treatment. It may be relieving and containing for both your child with BDD and for their siblings to know that all members of the family are held to the same boundaries and values.

There may be extreme cases where you or other family members may feel under physical threat by your child which can be very distressing for everyone. It is important to put measures in place to reduce the likelihood of this happening. Removing yourselves from the situation can be one way to do this, while ensuring your child is safe and not at risk of harming themselves. In some extreme situations, authorities such as the police or social care may need to be informed so they can intervene to keep everyone safe.

Managing family relationships

Sadly, BDD can become the centre of family life, directing what you can and cannot do. It is important to acknowledge how BDD impacts everyone and how it affects family relationships. While there is no one way to manage relationships, as they are highly complex, it is important to start thinking about the impact BDD has on each person connected and involved with your child.

You may wish to have a conversation about the impact BDD is having on everyone with individual family members or to sit down together and have a family meeting. The process of having these conversations can help each person to feel heard. There are likely to be parallels in what everyone is going through, and so these conversations can also serve to bring the family together. This can be especially helpful when it feels as though BDD is tearing your family apart. When having these discussions, it will be important that any blame for the situation is not attributed to your child. In just the same way as it is not your fault that your child has BDD, it is not their fault either. Try to remember that your child with BDD is almost certainly suffering the most in all of this, and did not choose to have BDD.

It may be helpful for family members who are struggling to understand your child's difficulties to read Chapters 1 and 2 of this book, or to look at the resources and websites listed in the Resources section. It is key that everyone has a good understanding of BDD and of what is happening for your child. To reiterate, it is important that blame is taken out of the conversation. We recommend, rather, reframing BDD as something the family are dealing with together.

You may have become aware that some individual family

members are struggling with the fact that your child has BDD. It can be helpful as a family to discuss what needs to be in place to ensure every family member feels supported. For example, if your other child (or children) is feeling neglected, it may be helpful to set out regular time for them to receive individual attention and time for them to do what interests them. You may find some family members need support outside of the family unit if they are struggling. They may need, for example, to access psychosocial support of their own like counselling or play therapy. In all of this, it is important not to forget yourself too! You can read Chapter 10 to get ideas about how to look after yourself.

Keeping your child safe

You may have read, or know from experience, that BDD can cause your child's safety to be at risk. This may include your child exhibiting hopelessness and suicidal thoughts, restricting their food intake, self-harming or engaging in risky behaviours to fix their appearance, for example, using abrasive products or trying self-surgery at home. You can look at the next chapter (Chapter 5) for guidance about how to manage hopelessness and suicidality.

If at any point you feel your child is unsafe or at risk, it is important to bring them to the attention of mental health services. Your child does not need to consent to this, as risk and safety trumps everything. If there is an imminent risk and it is urgent, you can take your child to the Accident and Emergency (A&E) department or emergency room (ER), where there are health professionals who will be able to assess your child. You may need to take your child there if there is a physical health risk too. If your child refuses to come to A&E or the ER with you, you may need emergency services to escort them. It is often helpful to flag up BDD to medical professionals as they may not be aware of, or know anything about, this diagnosis. If it is less urgent, you can contact your GP and explain the situation and again mention BDD when discussing your concerns. You can also share some of the resources in this book with them.

These steps may feel overwhelming but ultimately the goal is for your child to access the appropriate support. We know when young people access this support, they have a good chance of overcoming their BDD. It is important, as a family, to hold this in mind especially at times when you may feel you are taking drastic steps to access the support your child needs.

CHAPTER 5

Coping with Low Mood and Hopelessness

Although we appreciate this is a frightening subject, it is important to be honest and forthright about low mood and feelings of hopelessness in young people with BDD.

Research on BDD indicates that many young people with BDD struggle with low mood and feel hopeless at some point. Some young people will have thoughts about or may attempt suicide. Noticing signs of low mood, hopelessness and suicidality can be nuanced and very challenging. This chapter helps you to think about what you might pick up on if your child is feeling significantly sad or hopeless and how you can support them. It also includes some advice on how to seek the support of, and liaise with, other professionals and services if your child is struggling in this way.

It is important to note that feelings of low mood and hopelessness tend to be cyclical – to come and go in waves. It can be difficult to remember during the large dips of the wave that your child does not, and will not, always feel this way. Try to remind yourself, and your child, that all feelings are transitory and that no emotion lasts forever, however pervasive and difficult it seems to be. Offer your child reassurance that you are here to support them and that you have confidence the storm will pass. Try to avoid any messages to your child that they should suppress or 'push down' their difficult feelings; rather acknowledge the feelings of sadness, allow your child to express them safely in whichever way they feel able to, and then be ready to engage in an enjoyed activity together when the storm clouds have lifted.

Why are feelings of low mood or hopelessness often part of BDD?

Feelings of low mood can precede BDD for some young people. Some young people experience feelings of sadness and desperation and then project or 'pin' these difficult feelings onto their perceived appearance flaw or defect. They may blame extreme feelings of sadness, for example, on the 'fact' that their nose isn't straight enough or that their head is misshapen. Often, therefore, these young people wrongly believe that when their appearance defect is 'fixed' or removed their low mood will resolve itself also.

Feelings of low mood can also come as a result of BDD for some young people. The beliefs and behaviours that come along with BDD can drain a young person of their interest in life and of the fun-loving aspects of their personality. Some parents tell us they can feel they lose their child, for a time, to the BDD as their once cheerful child becomes depressed and anxious.

BDD is underpinned by pervasive feelings of shame and low self-worth. The experience of shame is very different from the experience of guilt in that shame typically feels all-encompassing. Guilt is the sense of 'I have done something bad', whereas shame is the experience of 'I am bad'. While it is possible to have feelings of guilt but appreciate that these are separate from who we are as a person, shame tends to permeate every aspect of the sense of self. These feelings of shame, themselves, can lead to a sense of hopelessness and despair.

Sometimes, young people with BDD come to feel as though their perceived defects will never be 'fixed' or acceptable, leading to a sense of hopelessness. They may also begin to realize that changing or 'fixing' aspects of their appearance fails to remove the pervasive sense of shame and desperation they feel. This can lead to deeper experiences of low mood and feelings of helplessness.

Warning signs that a young person may be struggling with low mood

The following are some possible indications or signs that a young person may be feeling hopeless and struggling with low mood. Of course, this list is not exhaustive, and the signs your child displays may be unique to them and to their experience. We recommend you go with your parental instinct. If you feel your child is feeling distressed and hopeless, they might well be. There is then an invitation for you to explore your child's feelings non-judgementally with them and to seek professional support and guidance. It will also be important to take any feelings of distress your child communicates to you seriously, not minimizing their emotions or saying things like, 'Don't worry. All teenagers feel a bit low from time to time.'

> ### Signs of low mood or depression in young people
>
> - Irritability and moodiness that seems 'out of character'.
> - Withdrawing from family, friends and regular activities.
> - Changes in eating and sleeping patterns (this might include weight changes, including failure to gain weight at expected developmental levels).
> - Lack of energy and signs of fatigue.
> - Feeling hopeless about the future.
> - Concentration difficulties.
> - Tearfulness and frequent crying.
> - Expressing feelings of loneliness and of 'not belonging' to their family, friendship group, etc.
> - Self-harm (self-injurious behaviour).
> - Thoughts of ending their life.

Sadly, suicidal ideation (thoughts of suicide) can be a feature of some young people's experiences of BDD. We appreciate that this can be a terrifying prospect for parents and want to assure you that, with the right help and support, your child's feelings of low mood and hopelessness can diminish and be replaced with positive thoughts and hopes for the future.

Risk, resiliency and protective factors

Every young person will have risk, resiliency and protective factors which will have a bearing on feelings of hopelessness. Resilience describes the ability to adapt to situations of adversity and stress, and to recover from these experiences. Both resiliency and risk are not static and depend on a range of both internal and external factors that might be present at any given time, such as the presence and encouragement of family and friends. Resilience can be fostered through and within relationships that are validating and supportive. Typically, a young person's resiliency develops through gradual exposure to challenging situations and experiences at a level of intensity that feels manageable.

For every young person, there are risk factors that increase their vulnerability and protective factors that can strengthen their resiliency. It seems that the more risk factors are present in a young person's life, the more they will require protective factors to counterbalance and enable their resiliency to flourish.

There are also a range of protective factors – factors which are known to reduce risk and may help with the low mood. These include, but are not limited to:

- Close friendships.
- Good problem-solving and coping skills.
- Social support from peers and parents.
- High self-efficacy.
- High levels of engagement in productive activities (e.g. school, hobbies).
- Attuned relationships and guidance from adults.
- Responsive educational environments.

Therefore, supporting your child and those around them to increase and expand upon their protective factors is likely to reduce feelings of low mood and hopelessness. This can be accomplished by:

- Supporting your child to make and sustain positive friendships (e.g. arranging for close friends to see them or call them; using social media safely to communicate with friends, etc.).
- Gently enquiring into and non-judgementally challenging any peer-related negative beliefs (e.g. nobody likes me, nobody wants to hang around with me, nobody would ever want to be my friend).
- Encouraging and modelling healthy assertiveness.
- Supporting your child to develop their problem-solving skills by helping them to think through possible solutions to experiences and dilemmas, trying out different 'solutions' and reflecting upon their outcomes together.
- Creating a safe space for your child to share their feelings.
- Preparing nutritious meals for your child and supporting them to eat a balanced diet.
- Supporting your child to have a good amount of high-quality sleep each night.
- Modelling positive self-talk and positive coping strategies as a parent.
- Encouraging extended family members to offer and provide support with the permission of your child. There may be a family member your child is particularly close to and to whom they appreciate talking through certain aspects of their experience. Although this can be difficult

to accept as a parent, some young people might find it easier to speak to a trusted family member or mental health professional than yourself about some aspects of their BDD experience. One young person explained to us:

'I couldn't speak to my Mum about everything because we're so close. Sometimes you need the people that you're not too close with to speak to. Because you have to face your parents too often. Sometimes you need to unload your struggles and just walk away with no consequences.'

- Educating your child's school about BDD (e.g. by providing them with leaflets, information from the BDD Foundation website, etc.).

Talking about low mood and risk with your child

Some parents tell us they are afraid to breach the subject of hopelessness, and particularly suicidality, with their child for fear that asking questions or talking about suicide will increase the probability that suicide will occur. This is a common and understandable fear. However, it may reassure you to know that there is no evidence for this in the research literature. Rather, the research suggests that young people who are able to talk openly about the topic of hopelessness and suicide with trusted adults are typically less likely to attempt to take their lives.

Speaking to young people about low mood/hopelessness/self-harm/suicide

☐ Listen, validate and acknowledge your child's suffering.

☐ Use active listening. This involves listening closely to what your child is saying, reflecting their verbalizations back to them through paraphrasing, and refraining from judging or offering lots of solutions in response.

☐ Do not focus solely on the feelings of hopelessness but ask open questions (questions that invite a response beyond a simple 'yes' or 'no') about why your child might be feeling this way.

☐ Be non-judgemental and, if possible, do not react with shock.

☐ Present yourself as confident and in control (however you may feel inside). For example, try saying things like, 'Let's work through this together to find a way forward.'

☐ Talk at your child's pace and give them time to talk at theirs.

☐ Don't make promises. Be realistic about what you can and can't do.

☐ Do not tell your child to stop thinking in this way; they may feel unable to do so.

☐ Ask your child what they want to do and how they would like you to help and plan the next steps together.

Here are some conversation starters you might like to try:

- [ ] I could be wrong, but it sounds like you are thinking about hurting yourself. Have I got it all wrong or is this right?
- [ ] Sometimes when people feel so distressed, they feel hopeless/think about suicide. Is this what you are feeling/thinking about?
- [ ] Are you telling me you are thinking of doing something to end your life?
- [ ] It sounds like you are feeling rather hopeless. Can you tell me more?
- [ ] Can you tell me more about why you feel so sad?
- [ ] It's hard and scary to talk about hopeless feelings but I am here to listen. You can take your time.

Informing involved professionals and/or seeking referral to professional services

It is important to share any changes you have noticed in your child's mood with the mental health professionals supporting them. Of course, if your child shares a plan with you to hurt themselves or to attempt suicide, you have a duty of care as a parent to share this with relevant professionals. Explain to your child that while you are able to keep most things they tell you confidential, anything that expresses the intention of harm to themselves needs to be passed on. Explain the reasons for this, reassuring your child that you love them and do not want to see any harm to come to them and explaining that part of your job as a parent is to keep them safe. It is likely that your child will already know this, even if they express disappointment in your trustworthiness at the time.

Having explained to your child that you will need to pass this information on, get in touch with any involved mental health professionals such as psychologists, psychiatrists, community mental health teams, etc., outlining what your child has shared with you and the extent of your concern. They should offer an imminent review and possibly also schedule a Professionals Meeting to collectively discuss ways forward. Ideally, you would also inform a key adult within your child's educational setting, for example, the Inclusion Manager, the school Safeguarding Lead or similar. It is better to have your child's agreement for sharing your concerns with others, although there may be situations where you have to share information without your child's expressed consent.

Possible routes of support

Your child might be offered medication (or a medication review if they are already on medication for BDD) if they are experiencing pervasive and distressing low mood. The prescribing professional should give you detailed information about any medication they suggest, including any potential side-effects. Do not lose hope if one medication does not appear to benefit your child (while holding in mind that an adequate 'trial period' is important and likely to be recommended, as we will explore more in Chapter 7). Sometimes a few medications may need to be trialled to determine which will work best for your child.

It might also be the case that changes or a deterioration in your child's mood prompt a change in the direction and/or pace of their BDD therapy also. For example, a therapist may decide to slow down the exposure exercises (which will be explained later), or to reduce their level of difficulty or intensity, during periods when your child is feeling particularly distressed or hopeless. During these times, CBT for BDD may be supplemented with other, broader CBT approaches to help your child (and yourselves as parents) to identify the thoughts, feelings and behaviours related to periods of low mood and how to best respond to and address them.

If there are not currently any mental health professionals involved with your child, gently persuade your child to come along with you to the GP (or to the Accident and Emergency department of your local hospital if they are distressed and share a plan to take their life). If your child refuses to come along to the GP, you could go alone on their behalf although it is better if they come with you. Your child might prefer to speak to the GP alone while you wait aside. Sometimes, GPs are willing to make home visits for special circumstances, and might find themselves speaking to your child through their bedroom door, for example.

If your child's distress levels are very high and they are sharing an expressed intent to attempt suicide imminently, and are refusing to come along to the Accident and Emergency department of your local hospital, you can call the emergency services and ask for an ambulance to come out to collect them. This is a very tough decision to make as a parent, yet a necessary one. While your child may feel very angry with you at the time, later they will be likely to come to understand why you did what you did and even to feel grateful for your decision.

A mental health professional will support your child in creating a Safety Plan or similar if they are expressing feelings of suicidality. A Safety Plan is a collaborative agreement made with and between the young person, family and involved professionals. It typically includes the elements shown in the box below.

Possible elements of a safety plan

- The warning signs of distress, including triggers and potentially triggering situations.
- The actions your child will take to maximize their safety, for example, letting someone know how they are feeling; refraining from being alone; focusing on a distraction task; talking to friends; obtaining safe sensory-based experiences (e.g. chewing gum, taking a warm bath, listening to calming or uplifting music).
- The actions the family will take to maximize your child's safety, for example, reducing access to harmful/lethal means; keeping the bedroom/bathroom door open; agreeing the frequency of checks if the young person is alone; spending time with the young person to openly discuss how they are feeling; supporting the young person to engage in their chosen distraction techniques/engaging in distraction techniques alongside them; giving the young person the contact details of helplines, etc.
- The actions others will take to maximize your child's safety, for example, providing a safe space in the

---

education setting; providing a named adult to talk to in the education setting; encouragement to engage in lessons and activities; reviewing the educational timetable as appropriate (the young person may need to be monitored in lessons within which harmful/ lethal products and implements are present); giving access to counselling and/or the school nurse; and building self-esteem through positive activity and responsibility.

Creating a Hope Box or Hope Book

Papyrus, the UK's leading charity for the prevention of young suicide, suggests making a Hope Box or Hope Book with young people who are feeling hopeless. This box is filled with things that help the young person to feel better. It doesn't necessarily need to be a box and could be any kind of container or bag. Some young people like to make little pocket versions (e.g. using a matchbox). The Hope Box should be personal to the young person, containing items they themselves have chosen. It can be enjoyable to decorate the bag or box to make it truly personal and unique. Some young people like to put soothing sensory items inside like squeezy balls, fiddle toys/objects, elastic bands to snap on the wrist, scented candles, lavender pouches, mints, popping candy, wind-up musical boxes and so on. The young person might also choose to include the numbers of their emergency contacts and helplines, a notepad and pen to write down how they are feeling, a list of soothing breathing exercises, a distraction techniques list, etc. For more information on how to create a Hope Box with your child, please see the excellent handouts from Papyrus, accessible on their website.[1]

Some young people will prefer to make a Hope Book, or might like to make a Hope Book to go alongside their Hope Box. A Hope Book follows the same principles as the Hope Box and contains images, photographs, poetry, quotes, music lyrics, magazine cuttings, theatre ticket stubs, etc. that make the young person feel hopeful. For more guidance, Papyrus have created a leaflet, also accessible from their website.

Reducing risk by amending the home environment

It is very important to take great care when removing from the home items your child may use to harm themselves with, especially if they have used a particular means before. It may sound extreme, but completely removing potentially harmful or lethal items from the home or keeping them in a locked safe may be necessary for a time. It is prudent to remove items related to means your child has used in the past, so that means removing all kinds of medication if they have previously made a suicide attempt using paracetamol; removing/locking away all sharp objects including razors, equipment in the shed/garage, etc. if they have previously used a blade of some description. There is a prevailing myth that if you take away one means of self-harm, a hopeless young person will use another. This is not what the research suggests. Rather, reducing access to lethal means

---

1   https://papyrus-uk.org/help-advice-resources

typically has a positive impact and, in many cases, reduces risk significantly.

Share the details of crisis helplines with your child

We recommend putting the details of crisis helplines (see the Resources section of this book for a list) somewhere your child can easily see and access them; this will also serve as a visual reminder of their existence. There are also hotlines you can use as a concerned parent (these are also listed in the Resources section).

Holding on to hope

There is help available for young people with BDD experiencing feelings of low mood and hopelessness. Research demonstrates that BDD treatment can very much reduce feelings of depression and anxiety and restore a young person's positive disposition and passion for life. As a parent, you can be a tremendous support to your child by listening to their feelings and worries, demonstrating empathy and helping your child to access the support they need, that is, in the form of mental health services. When asked what had helped him the most, for example, one young person shared with us:

'The morning after I talked to my mum about my BDD she sat there and said, "Everything's going to be fine." She's a big believer that if you draw up a plan it's going to work.

She drew up a little plan with me and said, "Tomorrow we're going to do this, we're going to the doctor." And that was a help and a relief to me.'

Another young person told us:

'Words the people supporting me used really resonated with and helped me, like, "We can beat this thing." I was like, "Oh my goodness, maybe I can! Maybe there's a life after BDD and that would be so amazing."'

At the heart of the matter of feelings of low mood and hopelessness is the need for the young person to feel understood, validated and loved. They may harbour a core belief that if their appearance defect is not fixed, they will always be unlovable: a terrifying prospect. Addressing the young person's core sense of shame and unlovability is absolutely key to reducing suicide risk in young people with BDD. This can be done in the home environment through many of the practices outlined in this book and through targeted therapies and professional support.

There is perhaps nothing as frightening for a parent as the fear that your child may be feeling hopeless and even contemplating taking their own life. We recommend making use of the Papyrus Hopeline and other available resources and having a read of Chapter 10 to consider how to keep yourself hopeful, healthy and nurtured in this most distressing of experiences. Try to hold in mind that most young people use a low-lethality means of attempting suicide with a high possibility of being rescued. Remind yourself regularly that many young people with BDD who have felt hopeless and engaged in suicidal behaviour have gone on to live happy and fulfilling lives. For ideas about how to support your child to live a life beyond BDD, please read Chapter 12.

CHAPTER 6

Supporting Your Child Through Their Education

'Every lesson I'd put my hand up to go to the toilet. Then I'd check my skin in the mirror and then go back to my lesson.'

(A young person with BDD)

This chapter will consider how BDD can impact on young people's education and access to work. It will look at some common barriers and challenges and help you to think about what you can do to support your child. It will also consider what 'good enough' support from educational settings looks like and what can be done to increase the setting's knowledge of, and improve their response to, BDD.

We know from the research, and anecdotal accounts, that young people with a diagnosis of BDD can miss a fair amount of school/college/university (hereafter referred to as 'school' for ease of reading). The attendance for some young people can become very low or sporadic. Others drop out of school entirely.

Some young people have shared with us the following reasons for finding it difficult to go into school:

- Social anxiety/social paranoia, that is, fear that other people (particularly peers) will see and judge their perceived defect.
- Fear of a repetition of the bullying/teasing they have experienced previously.
- Fear of certain lessons, especially PE and swimming.
- Not being permitted to use their 'camouflage', for example, not being allowed to wear hats in lessons or not being allowed to wear make-up in school.
- Not being able to engage in safety behaviours in school, for example, being unable to mirror-check during the school day whenever they feel the compulsion to do so.
- Fear of having school photographs taken.
- Fear of having to stand up in front of the class for presentations, etc.
- Fear of whole-school assemblies, fear they would be stared at.
- Perfectionistic tendencies that extend out into their academic work.
- Concentration and focus difficulties due to BDD-related preoccupations.
- Feeling that they are being punished by school staff, for example, for being late, for wearing too much make-up, etc.
- Fearing communal toilets, particularly those with mirrors.
- Experiencing rumours related to their BDD-related behaviours, for example, rumours as to why they are so often absent from school.
- Feeling that teachers/other adults do not understand them and are making assumptions about their behaviours,

for example, assuming they are late due to truanting or
being lazy.
· Finding the school environment academically pressurizing.

A leaflet has been produced by one of the authors about what
young people do and do not find helpful in the school environment, informed by conversations with young people experiencing BDD. It is available for download from the Resources section
of the BDD Foundation website.[1] You might also like to share
this leaflet with teachers and other educational professionals
involved with your child.

Supporting professionals to support your child

It can be incredibly worrying as a parent if your child is missing a
lot of school. You might even have the school attendance officer
and/or social services knocking on your door if your child is
missing significant chunks of the school term or academic year,
which can feel very intimidating and upsetting. You might even
have people making assumptions about your child, yourself and
your family because your child is turning up to school late each
day or missing a lot of school. One mother told us she struggled
with questions and comments like:

· Why is your child not in school?
· What's wrong with her? She seems perfectly fine.
· Take control of your kid.

---

1   https://bddfoundation.org/wp-content/uploads/BDD-Leaflet-for-Educa-
tion-Professionals.pdf

One young person shared with us the struggle of wanting to go to school each day, but feeling unable to:

'Every morning I had, sort of, this fight in my head of – you shouldn't go in, if you go in people will laugh at you, if you go in people are going to stare at you, people are going to be disgusted by you, you need to stay in bed. Yet at the same time, I really wanted to go. I really wanted to be at school. It was the driven part of me who wanted to be at school and wanted to push and make it in. Sometimes this would be stronger than the BDD for a while. Then, I think the BDD would just get the better of me and would suddenly become the one who was in control. I think it is probably because I didn't have the right tools in place – I hadn't had the BDD treatment at that point and didn't know what techniques to use to gain control again.'

We recommend having a leaflet about BDD, such as the BDD Foundation leaflet just mentioned, ready to give to professionals. Try to hold in mind that BDD is never any one person's fault and explain to professionals that you are doing the very best you can in very difficult circumstances. You might even like to keep a log or diary of your attempts to encourage your child into school, in addition to logging any meetings you have had at the school regarding your child's attendance and mental health. This can both provide evidence to explain non-attendance and also offer material to reflect upon when considering patterns in your child's attendance and professionals' responses.

Young people with BDD may miss education for a variety of reasons including taking a long time to get ready in the morning, depression (including finding it difficult to get out of bed), anxiety (particularly social anxiety), eating challenges (e.g. feeling weak from not eating enough), feeling overwhelmed by BDD, and being 'hung over' due to drinking a lot of alcohol (or experiencing the after-effects of non-prescription drugs) in order to numb BDD-related feelings and bodily sensations (this is more common in the later secondary, college and university years).

Young people have also spoken to us about experiencing high amounts of academic pressure: sometimes from school staff, sometimes from parents and sometimes from themselves. Some young people find secondary school particularly pressurizing. Of course, academic pressure is dealt with in different ways by different young people. In young people with BDD, any academic pressure on top of the BDD-related pressures they are already experiencing can simply feel like too much to handle. Academic pressure can feed into BDD-related perfectionistic tendencies also.

Unhelpful elements of education/schooling

Some parents find it very challenging to persuade their child to go into school each morning. This may lead to understandable feelings of frustration, even anger. It is important to remember that young people with BDD typically experience an internal battle of wanting to go to school but feeling unable to do so, despite the patience and support of their parents. Some young people have expressed feelings of guilt resulting from the impact of their BDD on their parents, which appears to add to their sense of shame. As one young person explained to us:

'The first thing I stopped doing was using the public school bus to go to school because public transport was difficult. So my mum started driving and some days I would make it to the school gates and then turn around and come back. I'd get my mum to drive me home and then I would say, "No, I want to go to school" and we would do a loop, back and forth, back and forth, sort of ten times each morning. My mum would ring the school up every day and say, "I am trying to get her in. Apart from literally dragging her and carrying her which I can't do, there is nothing I can do."'

It can be difficult for young people with BDD to concentrate on their schoolwork on account of BDD-related thoughts and preoccupations. Some young people may attempt to improve their concentration, such as by leaving lessons to check the mirror to try to lessen their anxiety.

Very worryingly, young people have spoken to us about feeling as though they have been 'punished' in education settings due to their BDD-related behaviours. They have told us they have received detentions and other punishments for: lateness, wearing too much make-up, leaving lessons to carry out safety behaviours, etc. Understandably, these punishments seemed to further compound their sense of feeling both misunderstood and rejected.

The pressure to attend school, on top of coping with BDD-related struggles, can seem too much to cope with for some young people. They may feel torn between wishing to go to school and feeling completely overwhelmed at the prospect of facing their teachers and peers. Some young people with BDD find attending particular lessons very challenging. PE and swimming are two of the most commonly avoided. This seems to be most typically linked to the fear of: removing clothing, wearing shorts and short-sleeved tops, getting the hair wet, putting the hair up and smudging make-up. Some young people with BDD specifically skip school on the days they have PE and/or swimming. Other areas of difficulty in the school day might include standing up in front of the class for presentations, walking in front of other classes for assemblies and having school photographs taken.

Very sadly, young people have told us that their teachers and other educational professionals have rarely asked them about the reasons behind their behaviours. This is one of the reasons why educating school staff about BDD is so vital.

Some young people with BDD miss exams due to BDD and/or find exams particularly stressful. We have found that they often appreciate having separate exam halls, having additional time for exams (to allow for 'breaks' when anxiety begins to rise) and having a reduced number of GCSEs/A-levels to contend with. Finding out about the protocols for access arrangements for exams in your local area and/or education authority will likely be very beneficial, for example, arrangements for your child to have extra time for exams, permission to take their exams outside of the school premises, etc.

Helpful elements of education/schooling

It can be difficult for young people who are missing large amounts of school to keep up with their schoolwork. Young people with BDD may appreciate schoolwork being sent home and missed schoolwork being placed on an online portal (to avoid them having to ask their peers). They may also appreciate extended deadlines for homework and coursework. Some young people with BDD may require part-time schooling and/or a flexible timetable for a period of time. You can have a conversation about these possibilities with the school inclusion team, educational psychologist or similar.

The approach taken by teachers and other educational staff can have a huge impact on young people's ability to cope and remain in school. Young people with BDD have told us they find it helpful to have a key adult within their education setting who is validating of their identity beyond their struggles. This seems to help them perceive a broader identity for themselves and to reduce feelings of being misunderstood and ashamed. Young people have also told us they find it helpful to have open lines of communication between their parents and their school, particularly in relation to absence. They tend to find it easier not to be asked by peers why they have been away after long absences. Some young people appreciate not having to go to PE and swimming lessons and being able to use this as study time for other subjects.

Some young people with BDD find college and university easier relative to the secondary school setting due to: having gaps between lessons, being able to be absent without getting into trouble, designated mental health services on-site, and peers being more open about mental health struggles at university. In terms of aspects of university young people with BDD find difficult, these may include finding it anxiety-provoking to live in halls with unknown peers, feeling lonely, university counselling services being too generalized (i.e. having no specialism in BDD) and the ramifications of regularly using alcohol to cope with their anxieties. One young person who had a very positive experience at university explained:

'I know many people have different experiences with uni in terms of BDD – it can definitely hinder it. But for me I definitely feel almost cured now. It was really good just to have a fresh start because I guess I felt like I hadn't really been able to just start fresh for a while.'

It is important to remember that there will not be a single person in the education setting who knows your child better than you do. While educational professionals have expertise in the area of supporting and educating children and young people, it is important to hold in mind that you have expertise and a lot of useful information to share with them in terms of your child's particular history, personality, likes and dislikes, fears, triggers and so on. It is clear that young people with BDD yearn to be understood, validated and empathized with in the education setting: to avoid further experiences of shame, and to have their identity recognized, esteemed and bolstered. You may be in a good position, in collaboration with your child, to support educational professionals in this process of treating your child with the understanding, dignity and respect they so very much deserve.

Actions schools can take, including adaptations

Simple adaptions to the school environment can make it much easier for your child to attend, to socialize and to learn. Some actions and adaptations within the school environment that can help for BDD include those shown in the box below.

Possible actions and adaptations within the school setting

☐ Staff researching BDD and understanding the complex reasons why the young person has been absent from school.

☐ Provision of key, attuned adults.

☐ Permission for the young person to approach key adults for support in their own time (while making it clear they are available) and non-judgementally enquiring about specific behaviours (e.g. refusal to take off their blazer).

☐ Taking a non-judgemental stance in general.

☐ Provision of a point of contact during absences.

☐ Thinking 'outside of the box' when considering points of anxiety during the academic term or year, for example, one teacher texted the young person to collect their GCSE results once the other pupils had left.

☐ Not publicly questioning 'unusual' behaviours (like leaving the classroom to mirror-check).

☐ Conveyance of a genuinely caring attitude.

☐ Provision of 'safe spaces' to go to when the young person is feeling dysregulated/distressed.

☐ Provision of a discreet means of the young person communicating that they need to leave the lesson and go to their 'safe space', for example, handing a card to the teacher, turning their homework diary over on their desk, an agreed hand-signal, etc.

☐ Identification of a list of 'early warning signals' with the young person and key adults – signs that they are becoming dysregulated, for example, touching their skin, rocking on their chair, eyes darting around the room, etc. Responses can be assigned to each signal, for example, when the young person is observed to be obsessively touching their skin, the teacher goes over and offers them a regulating activity such as going for a walk, sorting classroom equipment, squeezing a squeezy ball, fiddling with a piece of Blu Tack, etc. The Zones of Regulation approach and resources can be very supportive in this endeavour.[2]

Sadly, it seems that education staff sometimes notice worrisome BDD-related behaviours early on, but few ask curious questions about them. For all sorts of reasons, education staff may make assumptions about why your child is behaving as they are, without asking them open, 'why' questions, for example, 'Why do you always wear your blazer in my lesson, even in the hot weather?' They might assume that your child is wearing lots of make-up in order to subvert school rules, for example, or is coming in late to school each day because they (and perhaps you as parents) lack discipline and routine. It can help to invite education staff to be non-judgementally curious about young people's BDD-related experiences. Asking open questions, demonstrating empathy,

---

2   See www.zonesofregulation.com.

refraining from jumping to conclusions/making assumptions and supporting adaptations is likely to reduce the distress and sense of isolation felt by your child.

Sometimes it can feel difficult to 'give advice' to school professionals as a parent, perhaps due to a felt power differential. However, putting across your views and ideas about what would most help your child, including prompting education staff not to make assumptions but to ask yourself and your child open, non-judgemental questions about their behaviours, can be a very important way forward.

Some young people and educational settings find it very helpful to draw up an Individual Support Plan (ISP), which is a bit like an educational-setting based care plan. It can also be helpful for all members of educational staff to have a One-Page Profile of your child, which can be created in collaboration with key staff members, yourselves and the young person. Such a profile would include some key information about your child that all adults in the school should know about if teaching them or interacting with them.

Ways of supporting your child to attend school

Despite your very best efforts, it may be very difficult (some parents say impossible) to persuade your child to access all, or even some, of their education. It is very unlikely that you will be able to achieve increased educational attendance as a lone supporter – you will likely need the support of educational professionals and a therapeutic team.

It is recommended to request a multi-disciplinary meeting

if you notice your child is struggling to attend school, or is returning home from school distressed. This may include some of the following people:

- Class teacher/form tutor.
- Head of year/head of key stage.
- Involved school pastoral support worker(s).
- School attendance officer.
- Inclusion manager (sometimes called the Special Educational Needs Coordinator).
- Educational psychologist.
- Other educational professionals who work with your child or know your child well.
- External therapeutic support agents, that is, mental health professionals, therapists, etc.
- Family support worker(s).
- The young person – they may like to join at the end of the meeting, for example, if full attendance is feared or felt to be inappropriate. If the young person feels unable to come in person, they could be invited to offer their point of view to a trusted attendee of the meeting who can then become the young person's voice. Alternatively, they may like to write their views down to be read out, or to record their views using a dictaphone to be played at the meeting.

It is important to designate a Chair of the meeting and to set a clear agenda. If you are not the person setting the agenda, be sure to ask for a copy of this agenda ahead of time and make it clear what you wish to be covered in the meeting and what you hope the outcomes could be. Do not be afraid to question the purpose and agenda of the meeting if it does not align with what you feel needs to be addressed. It can be incredibly helpful to send a leaflet about BDD ahead of time to all attendees. Do not assume everyone has heard of BDD, has read up on it, or knows what to look out for and how to support a young person struggling in this way.

We recommend preparing notes before the meeting, as you may find yourself forgetting the key things you wished to say (even if you feel sure they are firmly in your mind). Clearly set out the points you wish to bring forward and tick them off, one by one, as they are covered. Write any questions down and bring these along also, requesting time to ask your questions at some point of the meeting, in case they are not covered as part of the discussion.

Even if someone has been designated to take minutes for the meeting, it can be useful to keep your own notes. This will also make it easier for you to both remember the key points of the conversation and to report back to your child (at a level matched to their emotional capacity) what was discussed.

An agenda for such a meeting might look something like this.

Possible agenda for an education-setting based Professionals Meeting

- Welcome and introductions.
- Overview of the agenda and desired outcomes of the meeting.
- Views of the young person.

- Views on reasons for difficulties with attendance, from the school and home perspective, for example, travel to and from school, bullying experiences, use of camouflage.
- Proposed support strategies/actions – including who will be involved in these.
- An opportunity for the young person (if they feel able) to share their views on the discussion and agree proposed strategies/actions and add any of their own.
- All present to sign the action plan. (Action plan to be disseminated to all involved parties.)
- Agree date for a review meeting (within a three-month time frame).

Involving an educational psychologist

It is very much worth asking the school if they have an educational psychologist (EP) available. Educational psychologists, sometimes called school psychologists, are specialists in supporting children and young people with learning, cognitive development, and social, emotional and mental health in educational settings. They are well versed in supporting schools, families and young people to come up with solutions where there are barriers to education, including mental health-related barriers. You can ask your school if they could make a referral for your child to be seen by the EP. Some EP services also accept referrals directly from parents and young people. Alternatively, you might like to seek out a private EP.

Particular reasons for involving an EP might include:

- The school communicating they are, or appear to be, struggling with how to respond to and support your child's needs.
- Involved professionals feeling 'stuck' in terms of finding ways forward.
- Your child receiving punishments for their BDD-related behaviours, such as detentions and fixed-term exclusions (a sign, potentially, that the school is struggling to understand, and respond appropriately to, your child's needs).
- A sense that adjustments may also need to be made to the school environment to enable your child to attend/ engage positively in their education.
- Additional support being required to support your child's transition back into school after a period of absence, including transition from a part-time to full-time timetable.
- A sense that your child may also have underlying learning/cognitive needs.
- A sense that your child may have social communication needs, possibly outside of, and broader than, their experience of BDD.

Thinking beyond mainstream education

While the aim should always be to support your child to return to mainstream education, for some young people fixed-term placements within an alternative provision may need to be considered. Alternative provisions often have much fewer pupils and a higher pupil-to-staff ratio. They may also be able to offer individualized learning plans and pathways. It might be that your child 'dips' into an alternative provision for a short while and then reintegrates into their mainstream school when they, and those caring for them, feel they are ready.

There are a few different types of alternative provision, some of which may or may not be available in your local area. Sometimes, young people will have to travel outside of their local area to access an alternative educational provision. Although travelling a long way to school/college tends not to be ideal for young people struggling with BDD for all sorts of reasons, this option should not be ruled out, particularly if you have identified a provision that you, and your child, feel will suit them very well. Some adolescent mental health provisions have specialist schools and if your child becomes an inpatient at any point, they may attend a hospital school on-site.

If your child is deemed to have a special educational need, which in the context of BDD may come under the social, emotional and mental health (SEMH) category, they may be placed on a kind of register depending on where they live, for example, the SEN Register in England. Depending on the policy in your geographical location, this may mean that your child remains under your powers of consent in the context of their education beyond the age of 16 (it can be up to the age of 25). They may be put forward for, and receive, an Education, Health and Care Plan (EHCP) or similar. Some suggested ways of utilizing additional funding/support include:

- Provision of a laptop to access missed work via an online portal.
- Providing on-site pastoral support (e.g. morning and afternoon emotional check-ins, or having a key adult free at key times to talk through areas of struggle/distress).
- Purchase of a bike/scooter and accompanying equipment if public transport is challenging.
- Provision of separate exam halls and personal invigilators for exams.
- Provision of alternatives to whole-class PE/games/swimming, etc. for a period of time.

We recommend talking to the school inclusion team or EP in your child's school, who will have an understanding of the process in your local area.

Holding on to hope about the future

It is understandable that it can be very anxiety-inducing to watch your child struggle to concentrate in school, to miss chunks of their schooling and to witness them potentially falling behind their peers both academically and socially. However, it is important to hold in mind that the brain is plastic (a term for the brain's ability to adapt and change) across the lifespan and that 'catching up' when your child is feeling better is both possible and achievable. With the right support, there is no reason why your child can't go on to achieve all they wish to achieve academically and professionally; it might just be a bit after their age-matched peers. It can be difficult for young people to come to terms with seeing their friends going off to university, for example, while they are spending hours each week in intensive therapy sessions. Your child will benefit from you holding positivity and future possibilities actively in your mind for them and reminding them of these aspects often. You may also like to enlist the support of parent partnership organizations or similar such as the National Parent Partnership Network,[3] and independent advisors such as Independent Provider of Special Education Advice (IPSEA)[4] in the UK.

It is possible to learn new things, to sit an exam, to get a degree...whatever it might be, at different ages and stages of life. Sometimes it can help to locate a peer mentor for your child – another young person who maybe had to 'delay' their education in some way due to mental health reasons and is now doing well in their chosen career. In this age of technology, you can also find examples of such people online; your child may enjoy watching their videos and hearing about how they came to their desired career 'later in life' and are so very glad they took the time they needed to get there.

Of course, we don't necessarily need to achieve degrees and academic qualifications to achieve our aspirations. The world and the job market are rapidly changing, and the education system quite simply hasn't caught up yet by any means. Whilst educational qualifications go a long way in some sectors, many people have 'made it' to where they would like to be without them. It can be really helpful to 'think outside the box' with your child about their broader dreams and aspirations and how they might go about achieving them.

---

3   See www.parentpartnership.org.uk.
4   See www.ipsea.org.uk.

CHAPTER 7

Seeking Treatment for BDD

In this chapter we will explore the recommended treatments for BDD. The more you know about, and are familiar with, BDD and the evidence-based treatments available, the more confident you will be likely to feel in helping your child to understand their difficulties and access the right support.

Available treatments

While there is no doubt that BDD can be a debilitating condition, it is important for you to know that it is treatable. Treatment guidelines, for example, National Institute for Health and Care Excellence (2015)[1] recommend two treatments based on the available scientific evidence for young people with BDD:

- BDD-specific CBT with Exposure and Response Prevention (ERP).
- High-dose selective serotonin reuptake inhibitors (SSRIs).

---

1   See www.nice.org.uk.

Unfortunately, sometimes young people with BDD are so convinced there is something wrong with their appearance they pursue cosmetic treatments like cosmetic surgery, dentistry and dermatology instead of psychological treatments like CBT. Cosmetic treatments like these are not a recommended treatment for BDD. It can be very difficult for parents not to accommodate their child's wishes, especially when hoping their distress may be relieved through physical procedures. However, research shows that when people with BDD undergo cosmetic procedures, they tend to be dissatisfied with, and upset by, the outcomes and/or go on to develop new appearance concerns. It can be extremely difficult for any parent to resist giving in to their child's plea for cosmetic surgery and similar procedures, even when knowing that refusal is in their child's best interest. Understanding the vicious cycle of BDD can help you and your child to talk about cosmetic procedures and their unintended consequences on your child's preoccupation.

Cosmetic procedures are physical solutions aimed at fixing the perceived defect or flaw in appearance. Whilst they may provide temporary relief, in the long term, cosmetic procedures maintain your child's focus on appearance. In treatment, parents are advised to find a time when both you and your child are calm and relaxed and free of obligations or distractions to talk about the consequences of cosmetic procedures and about your position as parents. This conversation is best avoided at times when your child's BDD-related distress has been triggered.

It is important for you to express empathy with your child's feelings while acknowledging your role and determination in supporting your child to overcome their distress and fears. For instance, you might say something like, 'I know you feel you really want me to take you to the dermatologist as you believe this will make you feel better. It must be really difficult for you to hear me refuse to support this. Perhaps you feel I am against you or trying to withhold something from you which you think is going to help. I want to assure you that I am on the same side as you. I will not take you to the dermatologist because I strongly believe it will not help you to feel better in the long term. My perception and belief is that you do not have a physical condition with your skin and that the sort of support we should be seeking for you is psychological support. I love you and know how difficult it is for you to hear this. I want you to try to trust me and to remember I am absolutely on your side.'

BDD-specific cognitive behavioural therapy (CBT) with Exposure and Response Prevention (ERP)

'I know that the first step in recovery is understanding that you've got BDD and accepting that.'

(A young person with BDD)

So far, CBT is the only psychological treatment that has been scientifically proven to be effective in the treatment of BDD in young people. Indeed, CBT for BDD has been tested in research and found to lead to a significant improvement in BDD symptoms and low mood.

CBT for BDD is a talking therapy that typically involves meeting with a therapist for weekly sessions of about an hour. A course of CBT for BDD usually involves between 14 to 20 weekly sessions depending on the degree of severity of the young person's BDD. The treatment often involves family members, depending on the age and maturity of the young person. Older adolescents, for example, may wish to have sessions without their parents. Nevertheless, it is important for parents to be involved enough to be able to support their child in between sessions, for example, with homework tasks. The essence of CBT treatment is to teach your child to challenge their thoughts and to change the way they think and behave in response to their appearance concerns.

Whilst researchers are still examining how to maximize and improve treatment outcomes for BDD, evidence suggests there are a few key stages to this type of BDD treatment. The first stage focuses on 'psychoeducation' and typically involves learning about BDD and the role anxiety plays within it. During this stage, you and your child will learn about what keeps BDD going, including how certain 'safety behaviours' (sometimes referred to as 'BDD behaviours', 'rituals' or 'compulsions') (e.g. mirror checking, grooming routines, camouflaging, avoidance) can fuel the appearance anxiety your child is experiencing.

In the second stage of CBT for BDD, your child will learn various techniques and strategies to overcome their appearance distress. Exposure and Response Prevention, or ERP for short, is the core component of the treatment for BDD in young people. While other CBT strategies may be used, these are typically employed to support ERP exercises or co-existing difficulties such as low mood. *Exposure* refers to deliberately confronting the feared or avoided situation that triggers the appearance anxiety. *Response Prevention* refers to intentionally resisting or reducing the safety behaviours. For example, it may include supporting your child to gradually reduce mirror checking before leaving the house or helping them to walk to the local shop without make-up.

Your child will receive lots of help and support from their therapist and any family members involved in their treatment as they gradually confront feared situations without engaging in BDD behaviours. After repeated exposure, the young person's fear tends to subside (a principle called 'habituation'). In other words, the young person finds the distress decreases over repeated attempts and they begin to think less about their appearance concerns in those situations. Alongside habituation and learning to tolerate distress, these sessions also allow the young person to test out whether their feared predictions come true (that people will notice, laugh or say something about their perceived flaw if they leave the house without their baseball cap, for example). For habituation to take place, ERP tasks and the skills learnt must be practised regularly in between sessions. As such, therapy homework is a vital part of a successful intervention. The role of parents in homework can range from reminding your child to do therapy homework to actively doing ERP tasks with them if they require encouragement and support through it. You can also help with keeping appointment diaries and support your child to access the therapy appointments. Of course, the relationship your child has with their therapist will be very important also. One young person told us that being able to have a joke with her therapist was instrumental in her recovery:

> 'I got on really well with my therapist and I felt that she understood me, and we could have a laugh. That's what I needed.'

You can support your child to build a positive relationship with their therapist by:

- Giving the therapist as much information as possible about your child's personality, sense of humour, likes and dislikes, previous family and friendship experiences, communication preferences, any social communication difficulties, etc.
- Keeping an open line of communication between the therapist and yourselves as parents, for example, informing them, ideally with your child's permission, of changes in your child's mood and behaviours.
- Keeping an open mind to the therapist's style and approach, while refraining from transferring any wider service-level frustrations onto the individual therapist or therapists (such as frustrations related to having had to wait a long time for treatment).
- Taking time to chat with your child between therapy sessions about what is going well and how their therapist is supporting them to make positive changes.

In some cases, parents may meet with resistance when attempting to discuss psychological treatment with their child. This often reflects the distress the child experiences at the idea of attempting to overcome their fear from a psychological perspective. In this and similar situations we recommend acknowledging your child's distress and combining empathy with an expression of your wish to help them overcome their difficulties, for example saying something to your child like, 'I know that going to the appointments is causing you a bit of stress but I'm so proud of you for sticking with the treatment programme. I am here to support you every step of the way.'

The final stage of CBT with ERP is about planning for the

future. In these sessions, the young person and their therapist, often with the support of parents, review all the tools and strategies learnt during treatment, and use them to create a relapse prevention plan.

Helping your child with BDD is a long-term process and may trigger all sorts of feelings including fear, helplessness and shame. Parents often feel guilty, like they have somehow failed because their child is suffering, and can struggle to know what to do or say. These feelings are an understandable consequence of caring for someone with BDD. What is important is for you to remember that *you are not alone* and *it is not your fault*. This situation can change once a child is diagnosed and educated about BDD. Diagnosis and education can often alleviate the fear and give hope that together, and with the right treatment, BDD can be overcome. Within therapy, BDD is named and the therapist can help to normalize your child's experience and provide guidance and support during the journey towards recovery.

Table 7.1: Key components of CBT for BDD

	Details of treatment components
Psychoeducation	Learning about BDD and anxiety/distress. Understanding what keeps BDD going, in particular the role of safety behaviours or BDD behaviours in fuelling and maintaining the appearance distress.
Exposure and Response Prevention (ERP)	Gradually and repeatedly practising facing the feared or avoided situations that trigger appearance anxiety, while reducing safety behaviours or BDD behaviours.

Relapse Prevention	Reviewing the main learning points in treatment and considering how to continue to build on the progress made.
	Creating a relapse prevention plan to stop BDD symptoms re-emerging and/or in case BDD symptoms re-emerge.
Additional CBT strategies	Additional CBT strategies can be used depending on the young person's specific difficulties and needs (e.g. mirror retraining, attention retraining, motivational interviewing).

'I mean, sure, CBT was incredibly difficult. In the beginning I had a lot of blips. It was really tough. But looking back on it now I feel like, even though it was challenging, it was rewarding as well. I have built control over BDD whereas it used to have control of me.'

(A young person with BDD)

High-dose selective serotonin reuptake inhibitors (SSRIs)

Treatment guidelines also recommend medication as an effective treatment for BDD, either alone or in combination with CBT for BDD. The type of medication used in the treatment of BDD belongs to a group called selective serotonin reuptake inhibitors (SSRIs), which includes sertraline (Seroxat), fluoxetine (Prozac), fluvoxamine (Faverin) and escitalopram (Cipralex) among others. This class of drugs is hypothesized to increase the levels of serotonin in the brain, resulting in a reduction or weakening of BDD symptoms and anxiety. Anecdotally, the medication can help to reduce the anxiety enough to enable a young person to fully engage in the CBT work. However, more research is needed into the long-term effects of combining medication and psychological treatments for BDD, compared to either treatment alone.

Medication should be prescribed and closely monitored by a psychiatrist or prescribing nurse within a mental health service. Many young people and their families have reservations about medication; it is important to discuss the facts and carefully consider the advantages and disadvantages of medication with a clinician. It will be important that you and your child have the opportunity to ask questions during this process and to take the time needed to consider the pros and cons of medication. Many concerns young people and parents have about medication can be addressed by discussing these issues with a psychiatrist. This should help you and your child to have a good understanding of what to expect, what the risks and possible side-effects are, and how to respond should any difficulties or concerns arise.

When exploring which medication to try, a psychiatrist will help you and your child to carefully consider all relevant information (e.g. your child's medical needs, medical history, medication history, potential side-effects, and any other relevant information). The prescribing doctor will generally start the medication at a low dose and increase it gradually over time to a targeted therapeutic dose. Research shows that for BDD, medications should be increased to a high dose, higher than for other kinds of difficulties such as depression. Although finding the right medication and dose for the young person might take some time, most young people will see an improvement after about four to six weeks of being on the targeted therapeutic dose. It is important to know that without an adequate trial, that is if a medication is discontinued too soon or the dosage is not high enough, psychiatrists cannot conclude whether a certain medication is the right fit or is not.

There can sometimes be unwanted side-effects from taking SSRI medication (e.g. constipation, dizziness, headaches). These will be monitored by the prescribing doctor. However, the side-effects typically occur within the initial phase of starting the medication and lessen over the course of a few weeks as the body gets used to the medication.

How to access BDD treatment

Often young people with BDD feel embarrassed to talk about their appearance concerns. They might be convinced there is something wrong with their appearance or think they are silly or vain for having these worries. They might also be fearful that if they share their concerns, other people may assume they are conceited. Young people with BDD, however, are not vain; they worry they are ugly or that there is something really wrong with how they look. Research shows that it can take an average of 10 to 15 years for sufferers to be diagnosed with BDD. To reduce the impact of undiagnosed BDD, early diagnosis and treatment are crucial. Supporting your child to share their appearance concerns with a health professional can be a big step in their journey towards recovery.

Your child's local GP is often the best place to start the process of finding appropriate help. The GP will be able to discuss the concerns of yourself and your child in some depth and to refer your child to your local Child and Adolescent Mental Health Service (CAMHS).

CAMHS is a multi-disciplinary team of healthcare professionals such as psychiatrists, psychologists and family therapists who are trained to work with young people (up to 18 years old who present with mental health difficulties) and their families in the UK. If the service accepts the referral it will offer an assessment, which will involve meeting with the young person and yourself to gather detailed information on your child's current difficulties. They will likely also gather background information such as a developmental history (i.e. historical milestones and events), education, peer relationships, interests, medical history and family history. Part of the assessment should be focused on gathering a detailed picture of your child's appearance concerns and other aspects of their mental health. Measures may be used to assess the extent and severity of their appearance-related distress, such as the Body Dysmorphic Disorder Questionnaire (BDDQ) for adolescents, the Appearance Anxiety Inventory (AAI) or the Body Dysmorphic Disorder Modification of the Yale-Brown Obsessive Compulsive Scale (BDD-YBOCS) for adolescents. The information gathered at the initial assessment will help mental health professionals to make a diagnosis and to offer appropriate treatment recommendations.

If a diagnosis of BDD is confirmed, mental health services should offer the treatment recommended by guidelines: that is, CBT with ERP and/or medication (SSRIs). An unfortunate reality is that some health providers will have limited resources, knowledge or experience of working with young people with BDD. As such, local mental health services sometimes refer young people with BDD on to specialist BDD services. For instance, they might decide to refer your child elsewhere if expertise in CBT with ERP for BDD is not available locally. This may also be the case if the young person is experiencing severe BDD or challenges that warrant specialist BDD treatment. These specialist services offer assessment and treatment to young people with BDD who are unable to access CBT for BDD locally or have not responded to previous CBT from their local or regional mental health services. NICE guidelines suggest a stepped model that involves going through local provision before funding for national services is considered.

Professional organizations and charities, such as the BDD Foundation and OCD Action, can provide support, resources and information on BDD, including advice related to accessing treatment, knowing your rights and options, etc.

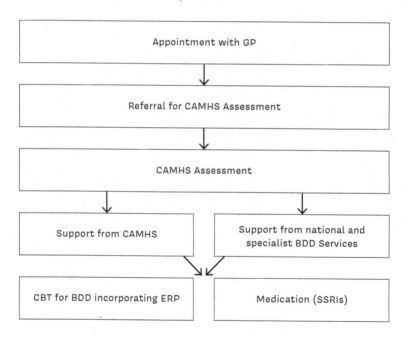

Figure 7.1: Flow chart showing possible path to treatment

Useful information to share with your
GP and other professionals

Most young people and their parents worry, to some degree, about what to say to a GP and how much to disclose. Young people with BDD might feel embarrassed and ashamed or might feel concerned about attracting unwanted attention to their perceived appearance flaws if they talk about them. An additional challenge to discussing BDD with health professionals is that they tend to be less familiar, and experienced, with BDD compared to other mental health conditions such as social anxiety disorder or depression.

Encouraging your child to share their appearance distress is often the first step in accessing the help they need. Your GP or mental health professional should be made aware of how time-consuming and distressing these appearance concerns are for your child and how much they are interfering in their day-to-day life. Sharing written information and resources that explain BDD in full and which describe treatment options with your GP/mental health professional can help to start these conversations and open the door to accessing the required support (for example, a GP Card about BDD is available on the BDD Foundation website in the Resources Leaflets section).[2] Self-report measures such as the Appearance Anxiety Inventory (AAI) or the Body Image Questionnaire (BIQ) can also be helpful in eliciting and discussing these difficulties further with the mental health professional. These can be accessed online, including via charity websites (e.g. BDD Foundation or OCD Action).

---

2   https://bddfoundation.org/wp-content/uploads/FINAL-GP-CARD.pdf

Here are some tips for supporting your child to share their concerns about their appearance with the GP or mental health professional:

- [ ] Help your child to make a plan about the information they would like to share and how to raise it, as well as which questions they might want to ask. It can be helpful to have these points written down to refer to during the appointment with the GP or mental health professional.
- [ ] Help your child to think about who they would like to be there to support them during the appointment (e.g. a friend, parent or family member) and what the manner of this support would ideally be.
- [ ] Take along with you any written documentation or resources that might be relevant to the appointment, for example information leaflets about BDD and information about the treatment options, as recommended by the treatment guidelines.
- [ ] Remind your child that the mental health professional is not there to judge them but is there to help and to think together with the family about how to best support them.

What to do when your child turns 18

In the UK, once children and young people reach a certain age, they are typically transitioned from CAMHS to adult Community Mental Health Services. This transition usually occurs at 18, but this may vary depending on the area and local teams. The transition to adult services can be a big and scary change for a young person and their families, especially if they have been used to working with their local CAMHS service over time. CAMHS should begin to discuss this transition three to six months before it's due to happen and will also help with the process of moving from one service to the other to ensure a smooth transition. For example, a CAMHS worker will typically arrange a joint meeting to discuss what ongoing support would be helpful for the young person moving into adult services. Sometimes the young person may not be eligible for the level of care adult services provide. In such cases, CAMHS will work closely with the young person and their family to make a plan for what will happen next.

Sometimes CAMHS teams will work with you to 'think outside the box' in terms of the transition from child to adult services. For example, one young person told us:

> 'I was quite lucky that the CAMHS staff realized I was going to turn 18 whilst I was an inpatient in hospital. The child and adult wards were obviously separate and it would have meant I would have had to completely change halfway through my treatment so they asked for my parent's consent for me to go straight into the adult ward because I was turning 18 within a couple of months. So, I was lucky enough to be in the adult ward at the age of 17 and turned 18 there, which was actually really, really great because it meant that my treatment was sort of linear and I didn't have to change partway through. My family and I were really happy my treatment was planned this way. It was really helpful.'

The importance of perseverance

We have spoken to many parents who have told us they witnessed tremendous leaps in their child's recovery when they received the correct treatment for their BDD. These parents tend to emphasize the importance of perseverance and persistence with medical professionals including GPs and mental health services and the necessity of not giving up hope if things seem to be moving very slowly. Don't be afraid to engage a mental health advocacy service if you feel your child is not receiving the assessments, treatment and support they require as you absolutely do not have to face the process of obtaining treatment alone. For parents' stories related to seeking and obtaining treatment for their child please see Chapter 11.

CHAPTER 8

Supporting Your Child Through Their Treatment for BDD

In Chapter 7 you read about the recommended treatments for BDD. In this chapter, we will discuss the idea of working together as a team during your child's BDD treatment. Parents are a unique asset and can act as co-therapist in supporting the therapy process. Here we will discuss some of the roles and responsibilities you can consider and agree on with your child and their therapist to support the key aspects of treatment for BDD.

Preparing yourself to be a co-therapist

Supporting your child through treatment can be challenging and bring about various feelings including fear, guilt, exhaustion and burnout. Indeed, BDD treatment can be hard work and requires a certain amount of physical and emotional strength and health. As such, it is vitally important you consistently take good care of yourself. We advise taking time each day to replenish yourself in whichever way you find helpful. This might be through meditating, listening to music, social support, physical exercise, spending time on your own or doing something you find self-soothing. However you decide to do this, the important thing is to remember not to routinely sacrifice your needs during the treatment journey. Please refer to Chapter 10 to read more about self-care.

Supporting your child in their struggle with BDD can be challenging and can bring about a range of reactions. Indeed, parents can harbour many feelings towards BDD, their child with BDD and/or the world in general on account of the challenges they face. Some parents tell us they feel angry, sad, hopeless and worried about their child. Some parents feel guilty for having these feelings and may not take the chance to acknowledge them. The truth is that these feelings are normal responses to a mental health condition that has been taking over your child's and family's life. It is important to give space to these feelings, acknowledge and perhaps discuss or challenge them with the help of your loved ones or your child's therapist, as these feelings may cloud your thinking and make it difficult to solve problems constructively. Some parents find it helpful to express their thoughts and feelings about their child's struggle in writing. They find this helps them to notice recurrent themes such as 'I should be able to fix it'; 'What if my child doesn't get better?'; and 'I feel helpless and don't know what to say or do to help my child.' Being aware of some of these thoughts and their impact can help you to gain perspective and prepare you to support the therapy process.

Helping to motivate your child

A major responsibility of parents is to help their child to access treatment for BDD. This might be achieved in various ways such as keeping an appointment diary, making relevant personal or work arrangements to access the clinic, and motivating your child to access help. Motivating a young person who is struggling with anxiety and BDD can be a challenge in itself, as often sufferers feel hopeless about change. Understandably, parents often feel responsible for fixing the BDD, but the harder they push for their child to have treatment the more the child might argue against it.

A first step is listening to and understanding where the hesitation about treatment within your child comes from (e.g. hopelessness that their situation is never going to change) and gently reminding your child of some of the things they might be able to do or accomplish should their appearance anxiety reduce. Reminding your child that therapy can help is important also. When a young person struggles to find any reason for engaging in therapy for BDD, parents can play a vital role in helping them to find reasons, set goals and agree on rewards for motivation. Remembering the starting point, noting the successes along the way and using praise and encouragement can be critical in maintaining motivation and confidence through the challenges of treatment. This may be particularly the case when engaging with the exposure exercises, which many young people find to be the most challenging aspect of treatment for BDD.

A helpful technique parents can adopt to foster motivation during treatment is that of looking back and looking forward. It is easy to forget the progress made and to focus on the things the child still finds difficult or cannot do, as opposed to what they can do. For example, a young person called Sarah felt overwhelmed by the anxiety related to the idea of working on reducing her morning grooming routine and attending school on time. Her dad also felt frustrated at her hesitation. However, both felt hopeful and encouraged when they remembered that just a few months earlier, Sarah would not have even considered going to the local shop without engaging in an extensive grooming routine. Now, not only was she able to walk to the local shop on her own but she could also interact with the clerk without engaging in excessive grooming rituals. Writing down the successes – however small – or the things the young person could not do before but can now do or face is a helpful way to motivate your child in continuing the hard work. Change is hard and effortful and the treatment requires great courage and perseverance. To this end we cannot emphasize enough the role of praise, words of encouragement and rewards as incentives to continue the recovery journey.

Supporting your child with the key facets of treatment

Psychoeducation
Educating yourself about BDD is crucial and is the first step in understanding what you and your child are dealing with. The first sessions of CBT for BDD will cover *psychoeducation* and will help you and your child to name and externalize the problem (to see BDD as separate from your child) and understand what BDD is, how it developed and what keeps it going. Your therapist will

be able to guide you through understanding the vicious cycle of BDD and answer any questions you may have. We always recommend being curious, finding out information, and doing research on BDD; various books, articles, online resources and videos are now available (please see the Resources section of this book and take some time to browse the BDD Foundation website). As people say, knowledge is power. Understanding BDD and its treatment will not only help you to empathize with your child's situation but will also likely increase hope and confidence in the treatment process. It will also enable you to provide guidance to your child when difficulties occur at home.

BDD is considered an anxiety disorder. During psychoeducation you will learn about anxiety, why your child feels anxious from time to time, how anxiety feels in the body when your child is anxious, and how anxiety can be rated. Anxiety is a normal feeling that everyone experiences at points in their life; it is an innate survival mechanism that helps us face danger by either fighting it or running away from it. A critical consideration for young people with BDD and their parents is to change their view of and response to anxiety. While anxiety feels unpleasant, it is important to acknowledge that it is temporary and is not dangerous. Situations that trigger anxiety bring about an opportunity for young people to learn they can fight back, as opposed to running away from the situation that has triggered the anxiety. This change can begin with you as their parent. Indeed, managing emotions and facing anxiety is an important strategy and skill that can be promoted through parents modelling behaviours to face their own anxieties.

In the initial sessions, the therapist and young person will create an *anxiety thermometer* to track how anxiety-provoking a certain situation or an exposure task is for the young person. Families can support this stage of treatment by practising using the anxiety thermometer with their child outside of sessions. You can also can adopt the approach personally and practise using a similar scale to track your own emotions during tough BDD moments to promote understanding and a shared language about anxiety.

Exposure and Response Prevention (ERP): overseeing practice and helping your child through successful work on exposure tasks

ERP is the key element of BDD-specific CBT treatment. It is important that parents understand what ERP is so you learn the language and techniques it involves. Your involvement in ERP will help you to empathize with your child's struggle and to learn how to support them through the challenges it involves.

Typically, therapy sessions will be once weekly. Engaging in therapy homework in between sessions is crucial to promoting and maximizing your child's learning and progress. To this end, you can play a key role in helping to oversee practice. The type and level of parental involvement will vary from child to child. It can range from reminding your child about exposure tasks or homework assignments, to helping them through the task, to simply being available if needed. During the initial treatment sessions, the therapist, young person and parents establish the level and kind of parental input desired and needed. We want the young person to feel in control and make choices as to what would be most helpful for them. This will help to foster the idea of working as a team and support your child to feel they are in the driver's seat of their recovery journey.

We recommend 'hands-on' assistance to parents for younger children. This might include attending every therapy session; promoting your child's understanding in sessions; praising and rewarding your child frequently for their efforts; and providing active assistance, for example with completing homework or monitoring anxiety, challenges and successes. With older teens and young people, the intensity of parental involvement may vary in treatment sessions. The therapist and young person would need to discuss the level of parental support desired and required each week for the therapy homework.

Whatever the level and type of parental input in overseeing practice and homework, you should always be informed of the current work and of weekly assignments and have a space to ask the therapist any questions and share concerns and important observations. Indeed, you may be able to notice specific challenges that only arise during homework tasks at home. You can then communicate these to the therapist and troubleshoot solutions with them in collaboration with your child. For example, sometimes parents observe that the exposure tasks are more difficult at home than in the clinic; this information can prompt an exploration of why that might be. It may be, for example, that the young person feels more anxious about doing the task in their local area and seeing other young people they know. The therapist can then make relevant adjustments so that the task in the session matches the level of difficulty required for the homework tasks. Sometimes, the therapist may conduct one or more sessions in the young person's home or hometown to support specific fears, safety behaviours and concerns.

Some young people find it helpful to make a *hierarchy*: a list of things they are afraid of, starting with the things they are most afraid of and finishing with the things they are least afraid of. Such a list can be drawn up for camouflage behaviours, for example, which the young person can incrementally work through, starting with the least fear-inducing item. An example camouflage hierarchy is given in the box below.

Taking the hat off when alone in the bedroom with the curtains closed.

Taking the hat off when alone in the bedroom with the curtains open.

Taking the hat off when around the house alone with the curtains closed.

Taking the hat off when around the house alone with the curtains open.

Taking the hat off around the house when other people are present.

Taking the hat off when answering the door to the postman, etc.

Walking to and from the local shops without wearing the hat.

Taking the hat off in lessons at school.

Taking the hat off in the school playground.

Reducing family accommodation of BDD symptoms

Families can become involved in the child's BDD struggles in various ways. We call this *family accommodation* as you read about in Chapters 3 and 4. Accommodation may take on various forms depending on each young person and their concerns and circumstances. For example, you may find yourself having to provide reassurance before the young person is able to leave the house or to participate in rituals such as checking your child's hair or the body part/s of concern to make sure it looks right. In other cases, the young person may demand that their family avoids specific places, activities or people (e.g. swimming pools, busy areas) and request them to change family routines to accommodate the BDD. These behaviours may keep the young person stuck in a vicious cycle uniquely centred on appearance worries and anxiety. You may have noticed yourself that at those times when you have provided lots of reassurance it increased your child's preoccupation in that moment. Or you may have noticed that your reassurance helped in the short term but next time a similar situation presented itself, your child requested the same, or possibly even more, reassurance.

In treatment, parents are asked to write down the ways they accommodate BDD symptoms and – using the anxiety thermometer previously discussed – to rate how difficult or anxiety-provoking it would be for you and your child to refrain from each form of accommodation. The aim in treatment is to gradually reduce each form of the accommodating behaviours.

Which accommodating behaviours are targeted, and how they will be addressed in treatment, will depend on their difficulty level and on their impact and priority for yourself, your child and the wider family. For instance, you may start with first working on refraining from discussing physical appearance at home, either in a positive or negative way, and focusing on attributes outside of appearance. You may then be able to move on to reducing your child's reassurance by choosing a time when it may be easiest to resist the reassurance seeking, including planning how to respond to requests for reassurance. You may respond to your child's requests for reassurance by saying something like, 'You may think I'm horrible, but I'm not going to feed into BDD by giving you more reassurance' or, 'I know this is really hard but I also know that reassuring you about how you look is not going help you in the long term.' This will likely be hard work for both you and your child and will require having to tolerate distress in the short term. You can help the situation by labelling and acknowledging the difficulty and anxiety and by reminding yourself and your child that you are dedicated to supporting your child to overcome BDD. Reminding yourself and your child that this will get easier over time can be very beneficial and anxiety-relieving also.

It is important to praise and reinforce the efforts you and your child are making at resisting safety behaviours, whether this be resisting family accommodation or resisting avoidances or BDD behaviours. Sometimes young people with BDD agree to something but then find it very difficult to stick with the plan if their BDD is triggered, resorting to avoidance or BDD safety behaviours. It is important to discuss this eventuality with any involved professionals and to prepare for it by developing a plan of action. With the therapist and your child, you can trouble-shoot the ways in which you can respond to pleas for reassurance or participation in BDD safety behaviours. Here are some things you can say if such situations arise:

Useful phrases when supporting your child in their recovery journey

☐ *Externalize the problem*: 'When BDD is triggered, anxiety takes over; don't let anxiety push you around.'

☐ *Empathize and make your child feel you understand this is a struggle for them*: 'I can see how hard this is for you, but I know you can do this; you have done so many brave things and I believe you can push through this too.'

☐ *Foster confidence and mastery*: 'I think you can win this one, let's give it all your best.' 'You can do this: short-term pain for long-term gain.'

☐ *Looking back and looking forward, remind your child of their previous successes, however small these might be*: 'You have been in harder situations than this one; remember when you did [insert example], you thought you'd never be able to do it but look at where you are now.' 'It was hard but you pushed through it and you have come so far already.'

☐ *Remind your child of their goals and values*: 'I know you really want to [insert example]. This will get you one step closer to achieving your goal.'

☐ *Remind your child that anxiety's main weapon is predicting failure*: 'Don't let anxiety push you around and tell you that you cannot do this; boss it back.'

☐ *Remind your child of what happens when you fight back or choose not to fight*: 'I know your anxiety is pushing you to [insert safety behaviour e.g. avoid, seek reassurance, etc.] but every time you fight back the anxiety is temporary and each time it gets easier than the previous one and you feel victorious.' 'Remember – when the anxiety takes over and you [insert safety behaviour], the anxiety gets stronger.'

Relapse prevention

The final sessions in treatment will focus on relapse prevention, including reviewing the key learning points in treatment and what has been helpful in getting better. Depending on how your child responded to treatment, the therapist and young person will consider what remaining symptoms may be left to work on and how to continue to work on these with the support of the family. As part of this process, a discussion should also be had about relapses. Even when significant progress is achieved in treatment, is important for you to be aware that relapses can happen and that they are normal and an expected part of gaining control over BDD. While we understand this may be unsettling to hear, it is also true that relapses are opportunities to practise what you and your child have learned in treatment. A plan of action will help anticipate stressful times when BDD symptoms might re-emerge (e.g. changes in medication, upcoming stressful events or transitions such as a change in school) and support you in recognizing the warning signs that things are slipping.

In relapse prevention, parents are an asset in praising and reinforcing their child's successes in treatment and reminding them of their ability to face the challenges in spite of their anxiety. Parents are also often helpful in identifying the warning signs that BDD may be re-emerging. Spelling out this parental responsibility to young people can help them to recognize the importance of this role and to understand why you may be vigilant or inquisitive about certain behaviours.

With the therapist you will develop an action plan which should include how you can support your child to fight back and regain control. This might include contacting the therapist if things become tricky again or helping the young person review what helped in treatment to get better. Regular ERP exercises are one of the best defences against relapses. You can help incorporate exposure tasks into your child's life or routine, including tasks that tie in with fun things, friendships and activities, all in an attempt to maintain or regain a full and meaningful life.

Supporting a young person when they are refusing all treatment

Some young people do not agree that their problem is psychological in nature and may reject all treatment for BDD. It is possible that a young person's BDD may deteriorate through continuing to refuse treatment. Their suffering may reach the point where they threaten harm to themselves or others and may be considered at risk. This is a very challenging situation for everyone involved and may require consideration of inpatient treatment. In such cases, safety will be the primary focus and inpatient treatment options should be discussed thoroughly with your local mental health service and professionals involved in your child's care. The BDD Foundation provides information on inpatient facilities that provide BDD treatment in the UK. Feel free to return to Chapter 5 to read more about responding to risk in the context of BDD.

Even if your child may not be in need of inpatient care, seeing your child suffering and not knowing how to help can a very difficult situation for parents of young people who refuse all treatment for BDD. The hard truth is that BDD treatment requires your child's effort and input. Therefore, young people cannot and should not be forced into treatment. Forcing treatment will likely only increase conflict and resentment for both you and your child. Nonetheless, even if the young person is not ready for treatment, there are things you can do as a parent. Although such things cannot guarantee you will change your child's view of, or change their mind about engagement in, treatment, they may allow you to remain on the same side whilst also over time increasing the chances that your child may come around to the idea of specialist input and support.

One of the key pieces of advice is to express your hope and confidence to your child that treatment can help. When you see your child struggling with BDD, empathize with their anguish and remind them that treatment is available and may be a way out of their suffering. For example, when noticing her suffering, Victoria's parents let her know that they were ready to get her the help she needed if and whenever she felt ready for it. They didn't argue with or push her, but rather honoured her decision and gently reminded her that help was available and that they were ready to support her to access it whenever she was ready to do so.

While the young person may not be ready or agree to embark on CBT for BDD, parents and family members can still work on reducing family behaviours that accommodate BDD symptoms.

This can help to address some of the behaviours that maintain and exacerbate BDD. It can also model a family culture which encourages everyone to find solutions and work through them together despite the challenges.

It may be possible to involve a therapist even if your child is refusing to engage in treatment. In this instance, the therapist would be supporting yourselves as parents to support your child. The therapist can help, for example, to create a gradual plan towards reducing family rituals or avoidances, including a timeline. It is important to make small, gradual and predictable steps towards reducing accommodation and to avoid withdrawing family participation and avoidance abruptly. Providing the rationale for accommodation withdrawal, alongside giving plenty of warning to your child as to what will happen and how, will help them to be prepared. Sometimes reducing family accommodation also helps a child who refuses treatment to recognize the extent of their difficulties and strengths. They may recognize that they can cope with the distress of BDD not being accommodated by family members or, at other times, notice that it might increase the burden and highlight the need to keep working hard towards recovery.

We have successfully worked with many young people who initially refused treatment for their BDD. This highlights the importance both of patience and of holding on to hope as parents. We recommend continuing to work on reducing your family's accommodation of your child's BDD and to regularly remind your child that treatment is available when they are ready for it. You may be pleasantly surprised by your child's seemingly sudden change of heart and willingness to engage in the treatment process.

CHAPTER 9

Supporting Your Child in Navigating the Internet and Social Media

'I would be shut up in my room quite a lot. I'd often be online doing things like researching plastic surgery, going on social media comparing myself, you know all that kind of stuff.'

(A young person with BDD)

In this chapter we will consider the impact of the internet, and particularly social media, on BDD as well as discussing a few strategies to help you and your child to navigate social media and reduce its possible negative effects on body image and appearance anxiety.

Before we embark on this chapter, we feel it is important to highlight that there is no evidence to suggest social media is a causal factor in BDD. While social media can certainly have a negative impact on young people, on their perception of their appearance and on their BDD, BDD is far more complex than a direct response to social media influences alone. There is far more evidence, for example, that traumatic experiences like bullying are possible causal factors in BDD (e.g. Neziroglu *et al.*, 2018; Weingarden *et al.*, 2017).

Cyber-bullying and BDD

There are no studies which have directly explored possible links between technology and BDD. There are studies, however, which demonstrate that bullying and teasing experiences are more common in young people with BDD than in the general population (e.g. Neziroglu *et al.*, 2018; Weingarden *et al.*, 2017).

Cyber-bullying is a kind of bullying that takes place through technology. Some of the bullying young people with BDD may experience or have experienced in the past may have taken place either partially or entirely online and/or via mobile messaging. It is important to note that the methods used by young people who bully others online tend to be hidden and subtle. Of course, cyber-bullying can worryingly be perpetrated by adults towards children and young people also. Frighteningly, adults may masquerade as young people online (including by posting false photographs and dates of birth) and parents should be aware that if the person bullying your child online is not known to them in the real world, they may be an adult and a serious safeguarding concern may be present. If you have any evidence for such an occurrence, it will be important to inform both the platform on which the bullying is taking place and the police.

Cyber-bullying can be a particularly virulent form of bullying as it can take place 24/7 and affect a young person anywhere there is internet or data access, including in their bedrooms in their own homes. Cyber-bullying can also escalate more rapidly than other forms of bullying as multiple messages can find their way to a young person's device in very short spaces of time. In some of the newer apps like Snapchat, any evidence that the cyber-bullying took place is lost. For those who experience it, cyber-bullying can be an utterly consuming and unrelenting experience which can be difficult to share with others.

If you suspect your child is a victim of cyber-bullying, or has been in the past, we recommend inviting an open conversation with your child about their experiences. Considering how any bullying experiences may have contributed to their BDD is always important and is a process that can be supported by the mental health professionals working with your child. As part of any conversation you have with your child it will be important to emphasize that any bullying they have experienced, either online or otherwise, is not their fault. Reassure your child that they have done the right thing by speaking to you about it.

It is important to make sure your child knows how to block anyone who is being unkind to them through each app or online service they are using. Details of how to do this can usually be found in the 'Help' or 'Online Safety' area, under the 'Settings' of each platform, service or app. You can also report, and/or support your child to report (if it is age appropriate and they feel able to do so), anyone who is bullying your child to the platform who carries or carried the offending material. Whether or not the perpetrator(s) attends the same educational setting or club as your child, it will be important to discuss sharing this information with your child's teacher/head of year/ pastoral support worker/club leader, etc. as other young people in that setting may also be vulnerable or be experiencing the same thing.

Unfortunately, the evidence suggests that only around 38 per cent of cyber-bullying is ever reported to parents.[1] By regularly checking in with your child and scheduling in time for open, non-judgemental conversations about anything that might be bothering them, you will be making it easier for your child to share difficult experiences like cyber-bullying with you. If they have already disclosed, encourage your child to tell you if any new incidents of bullying occur and keep a written record of these. Your child might also find it comforting to contact external support such as Childline in the UK, who can advise young people of how to respond if bullying, including cyber-bullying, is going on.

While cyber-bullying is not specific to BDD, we felt this section was important to include as we know bullying experiences can precede BDD for many young people. Even if your child is telling you about the bullying some time after the event, conversations can still take place and actions still be taken. Sharing any disclosures made about bullying experiences by your child with any mental health professionals working with them will enable targeted therapeutic support to be planned and delivered addressing this specific area.

See the box on the following page for ways in which you can support your child to take steps to prevent cyber-bullying.

---

1   Techjury cyber-bullying statistics (2019): see https://techjury.net/stats-about/cyberbullying/#gref.

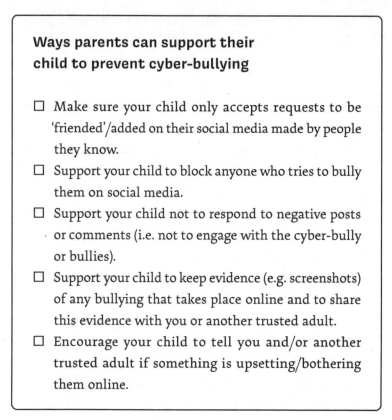

Ways parents can support their child to prevent cyber-bullying

☐ Make sure your child only accepts requests to be 'friended'/added on their social media made by people they know.

☐ Support your child to block anyone who tries to bully them on social media.

☐ Support your child not to respond to negative posts or comments (i.e. not to engage with the cyber-bully or bullies).

☐ Support your child to keep evidence (e.g. screenshots) of any bullying that takes place online and to share this evidence with you or another trusted adult.

☐ Encourage your child to tell you and/or another trusted adult if something is upsetting/bothering them online.

Media use in BDD and its impact on BDD symptoms

We would like to acknowledge the fact that – when used with caution – there are undoubtedly many benefits to using the internet and social media, not least the vital role they can play in educating and connecting young people. Some studies have demonstrated a positive link between social media and body image, given the potential to combat unrealistic appearance ideals by promoting more realistic images, for example through campaigns such as #nomakeup and #nofilter.

To date, no research has examined, and therefore established, a causal link between internet and social media usage and BDD. Nonetheless, we know that people who suffer from appearance anxiety or BDD can use the internet and social media in a way that fuels their appearance concerns. For example, BDD sufferers often spend extensive amounts of time:

- Scrutinizing and comparing their appearance with others, for example on sites like Instagram, Facebook and other image-centric apps.
- Searching online for products, cosmetic procedures or remedies in a desperate attempt to 'correct' or 'better' their appearance. For example, one young person explained to us:

'I read online that because nose is made of cartilage and not bone you can re-mold it or something which is probably not true. I don't really know but you read all this stuff online. So I would spend two half-hour periods a day, sort of like pushing the palm of my hand into my nose to try and change the shape of it.'

- Seeking reassurance about their appearance online, for example by uploading photos on websites where appearance is rated.

Image-centric apps such as Instagram and Facebook can promote repeated and compulsive scrutiny of one's own and others' appearance. Often the primary emphasis on social media platforms is on how one looks. These platforms can promote a sense of self-worth based on likes and comments based at least partially on appearance. The risk with such use of the internet and social media in BDD is that it can keep the young person stuck in a vicious cycle solely centered on appearance, all the while magnifying those beliefs and feelings of personal inadequacy and flawed-ness.

Reducing screen time may be part of the ERP element of CBT for your child during BDD treatment, particularly if they are compulsively taking selfies, spending hours online researching cosmetic surgery/dentistry/dermatology and/or seeking appearance-focused reassurance on online forums and similar. Your child could be encouraged to use app trackers to log their time spent online to ascertain how much each app is used. You can also support your child to download apps which tell them how much time they spend on their phone/electronic device and help them to begin to reduce the time spent on their devices. For example, you and your child can set a designated amount of time on their device and, when they have reached their limit, they will no longer be able to access the apps they have been using. As a parent you can be a very important support agent in this endeavour, helping your child to research and install such app trackers and celebrating their progress in reduction of their use of these apps, however small. The use of trackers can also highlight the times of the day and week the young person is spending most of their time online engaging in BDD-related behaviours. This can provide useful information about the times your child is struggling the most and may require more support. Sharing information about your child's patterns of internet and social media usage with any involved professionals, particularly if it appears to be feeding into their BDD, is strongly recommended.

Of course, if your child is working on reducing their time

engaging in BDD-related behaviours online, they will require something to fill this time. The danger is that this additional time could be used to engage in BDD-related behaviours in other ways, for example, mirror checking, skin picking, etc. Therefore, it will be important to think with your child, coupled with the support of involved professionals, about what they will be doing with the time they would ordinarily be spending online. It might help to draw up a clear timetable to include enjoyed activities and hobbies. Here are some ideas of alternative activities to the use of technology, some of which you or other family members or friends may be able to undertake with your child.

Ideas for activities to replace screen time

☐ Playing a musical instrument.
☐ Stroking, brushing, grooming and playing with a pet.
☐ Engaging in creative writing.
☐ Drawing or painting a picture.
☐ Making a collage from old magazines, etc.
☐ Engaging in mindful colouring (you can now buy many mindfulness colouring books with various themes).
☐ Watching an uplifting movie.
☐ Weaving, knitting or crocheting.
☐ Doing a jigsaw puzzle with many pieces.
☐ Reading a book or listening to an audio book.
☐ Baking a cake, making jam, etc.

Portrayal of unrealistic appearance ideals in the media

Another issue that requires addressing is the vast number of images and unhelpful messages about appearance we are all confronted with daily, whether this be online, in magazines, on TV or in adverts. These images and messages can affect young people's body image detrimentally. Indeed, the images often portrayed tend to be unrealistic and unattainable; they have often been carefully selected and heavily edited through digital filters, Photoshop and other means. These images do not represent the general population and are far from realistic. These images of 'perfection' can exacerbate appearance anxiety and the urge to find solutions to 'correct' or 'better' one's appearance.

Unfortunately, we are flooded these days with many unrealistic images which sell us an unreachable physical ideal and tell us how to achieve it. One ramification of the unhealthy pressure to achieve an 'ideal image' is the increase in young people seeking cosmetic treatment and asking for procedures to look like their Snapchat filtered selfie, for example. When it comes to BDD, those images and messages are likely to perpetuate low self-esteem, a sense of worthlessness and feelings of inadequacy, all of which can feed into an endless search to reach these physical ideals.

What parents can do to help their child navigate social media and other appearance influences

Parents can play an important role in increasing their child's awareness of the online body-image messages and in helping to minimize the negative effects of these images on BDD symptoms.

Leading by example can be very effective in supporting your child away from the more negative aspects of the internet and social media. Becoming more aware of your own internet and social media usage, including how often you are 'checking' and scrolling with your phone and other devices, can go a long way in modelling a healthier relationship with technology to your child. By cutting down on your own screen time, you will be likely to inadvertently encourage your child to do the same, particularly if they are spending a lot of time with you. You can also actively delete or 'unfollow' unhelpful appearance-related influences, explaining to your child why you have chosen to do so. Of course, less screen time makes more time for relational connection, which will be vital to your child as they struggle through the vicissitudes of BDD.

Setting clear boundaries for your child can help reduce exposure to social media that may exacerbate BDD symptoms. This might include establishing which internet sites and social media platforms are safe and age-appropriate and supporting your child to put/accept blocks on their phone and other devices to keep them safe as previously described. Parents can monitor and discourage the use of sites that are unhealthy, such as those where young people upload their picture for appearance to be rated by strangers. Setting time limits or times when phones should not be used, such as during mealtimes, for example, is another way parents can help monitor healthy online use.

Some families choose to have 'digital detoxes' as a whole family, spending a whole day or even a weekend or longer without phones and other electronic devices. If this is a whole-family affair, no individual is likely to feel singled out and the family can have a chance to spend time together in other ways, such as chatting, playing board games and so on. Other families have clear curfews, such as that the internet and access to all devices ends at 9pm. Adequate sleep is absolutely vital to your child's mood and wellbeing and, therefore, to their recovery from BDD. The recommendation is to switch off all electronic devices or anything with a screen *at least two hours* before bedtime. It will be important to activate any features that keep your child's mobile phone from emitting blue light at night if they are going to keep their phone in their bedroom. In fact, we recommend encouraging your child to remove their phone and other electronic devices from their bedroom at night to promote a higher quality of sleep. Your child may find this easier to agree to if the whole family adopts the same practice, perhaps with everyone putting their phones/devices into a box in a separate room of the house before bed.

We feel it is important to invite open conversations with your child about body image and social media. For example, we suggest that parents take time to discuss with their child why and how many images are considered unrealistic, while helping the young person to recognize the vicious cycle of social media and its effect on their appearance anxiety. We recommend that you regularly remind your child that social media does not show an accurate picture of people's appearance and their lives and that people's self-worth should never be based entirely on their looks, likes or followers. You can also model and help to counterbalance the effects of negative body-image messages online by redirecting conversations away from appearance and emphasizing what bodies can do as opposed to what they look like (i.e. emphasizing the functionality of bodies over their form). You can also encourage your child to balance their screen time with positive and constructive online forums with a reduced emphasis on appearance, where other traits and values are prioritized.

We'll leave you with an acronym suggested by *Psychology Today*: remember **F-A-C-E** when talking about social media with your child:

- **F**ilter – support your child to filter the media they are exposed to. Body image researchers sometimes refer to this as 'protective filtering'. Essentially, any social media that is proving to be harmful to your child's self-esteem and wellbeing should be filtered out. If an app or platform makes your child feel consistently bad about themselves, they should be encouraged to drop the app to keep themselves from feeling so bad in the future.
- **A**void – support your child to avoid some social media some of the time. This includes encouraging real-world interactions and evading unwanted online interactions. Avoiding responding to negative comments on social media is an important aspect of this also.
- **C**areful of comparisons – support your child to be careful about making any comparisons online, for example, comparing a body part to the body part of an online photograph. Remind your child that social media is *not* an objective and reliable source of information.
- **E**valuate – support your child to evaluate how they are spending time on social media. Remind your child regularly that many online images are filtered, edited and enhanced in a variety of ways.

It is also helpful to hold in mind, as we mentioned at the beginning of this chapter, that many young people discover and use positive aspects of the internet and social media, including within their recovery journey from BDD. Young people have told us about how connecting to other young people online has supported their recovery journey, including through sharing their experiences of BDD as a way to raise awareness and support others through their experiences. We'll also leave you with the reflections of one young person with the caveat that young people will almost certainly require support to manage any 'backlash' from any sharing on social media they engage with:

'Obviously, sharing your journey with BDD on social media is really difficult to do. But the reason I do it is because I had never heard of BDD. If I had heard of BDD earlier, I might not have gone through that couple of years just not knowing what I was dealing with. That's why I do the media awareness because I think if it just helps one person like me then that's worth it. I am really pleased I have done it and I continue to take any opportunity I get. However, I do need to be aware of putting my mental health first because one thing with my BDD is that I am a bit of a people-pleaser. So sometimes I say yes to media awareness stuff to try to please others. So sometimes I need to be careful and not just agree to things because I feel bad. I have to do it because I want to do it, which I'm sort of getting better at.'

CHAPTER 10

Self-Care for Parents

This chapter considers the importance and necessity of self-care for parents of children struggling with BDD. It offers practical advice on how to manage anxiety and to make self-care a part of your daily routine, regardless of limited time and available resources. It also explores ways of enlisting the support of trusted others.

Parents of children and young people with BDD experience multiple additional stressors as well as the everyday strains of being a parent. In addition to worrying about your child's emotional state and quality of life, you may also have to exert considerable effort in finding and securing psychosocial treatment for your child (and perhaps for the whole family). You may need to liaise closely with school professionals to make school easier (or even a possibility) for your child. You may have to juggle the experiences and emotions of other members of your family also.

As we have highlighted at various times throughout this book, sometimes parents even blame themselves for their child's struggles. It is very important to be clear that BDD is not your fault and the attribution of blame and guilt is likely to be very painful and hugely unhelpful. BDD is a complex experience that is influenced by a range of interwoven and inter-linking factors. Taking the full responsibility for your child's BDD will likely be detrimental to not only your own mental and emotional health but also that of other family members.

Letting go of guilt

Letting go of perceived guilt is, of course, easier said than done. It can help to acknowledge what you feel your part in your child's BDD has been, and to then communicate this to a trusted person such as a family member or a friend with the emotional capacity to listen to you without making judgements. You might decide to seek some counselling for yourself, or another form of psychosocial support.

The first step in letting go of feelings of guilt is to make a strong commitment to yourself to do so. This commitment will likely need to be repeatedly renewed, perhaps many times each day, to ensure you do not slip back into old ways of thinking, that is, becoming saturated in an inner dialogue that is critical of, and unkind to, yourself. Fostering self-compassion is vital to this commitment and this process. Here are some ideas for fostering self-compassion, thus supporting you to let go of feelings of blame and guilt:

☐ Reflect on what the concepts of kindness and self-com-passion mean to you. Consider looking into the work of compassion-focused clinicians like Paul Gilbert

(2009, 2010) and Kristin Neff (2011). You might like to collage a kindness or self-compassion picture from magazines, etc.

☐ Place the focus of your attention on what it would feel like to be filled with self-compassion. How would you think, feel and act? Consider what facial expression you would associate with this self-compassion and bring this expression to your face. Consider what posture you would associate with this self-compassion and move your body into that posture. In this way, you begin to embody this sense of kindness to yourself.

☐ Imagine a colour associated with compassion and kindness. Imagine this colour surrounding you, then entering into you through the pores of your skin, slowly spreading throughout your whole body and particularly coming to rest in the area of your heart.

☐ Think back to a time when you extended compassion to another. Turn these feelings of compassion towards yourself.

☐ Extend loving and compassionate thoughts to yourself, for example, 'May I be well', 'May I be peaceful', 'May I feel my own goodness'.

☐ Imagine an anxious, shameful and self-critical version of yourself and a kind, self-compassionate version of yourself. Embody the sense of your self-compassionate self and extend love and warmth to your self-critical self.

Acknowledging yourself as a protective factor

Sometimes parents of young people with BDD feel they have become disconnected from their child and that they no longer know how best to support them. There can even be the sense that their child no longer trusts them or feels angry with them all the time, as young people with BDD often struggle to understand why their parents deny seeing the perceived defects, feeling others are lying to them. Your child may be frustrated that you will not agree to the cosmetic surgery they are seeking, for example, or become angry with you for not offering reassurance in the way they want it, as frequently as they want it.

As a parent, it can feel as though you are stuck between a rock and a hard place, wanting to make your child feel better but not wanting to feed into the preoccupations and obsessions that are part-and-parcel of BDD. Please feel free to return to Chapters 3 and 4 to remind yourself of strategies for dealing with challenging and possibly aggressive behaviour related to your child's struggle with BDD.

Amidst this confusion, it can be difficult to hold on to the fact that you are a protective factor for your child (you really are!). What this means is that your presence and support can both reduce and diminish the likelihood that your child's BDD will continue to rule their life, which is often how it can come to feel. The more emotionally stable, centred and mentally strong you are, the more possible it will be, and feel, to do this. The methods and practices presented in this chapter aim to support you in this endeavour.

Make self-care a part of your everyday routine

Parenting a child with BDD can very much mean that your own self-care goes out of the window. While this is completely understandable given how utterly absorbing BDD can become for the whole family, it is also neither sustainable nor beneficial. Making self-care a part of your daily life is not only recommended but, we feel, essential. While this might feel impossible given how much you have to worry about, organize, monitor and so on, we would like to put it to you that self-care is always possible and would ideally become a priority for you. We hope some of the following suggestions might feel doable.

We recommend that you set some time for yourself, perhaps 20 minutes, to do something for yourself daily. Here are some ideas of what you might do:

Suggestions for self-care

☐ Breathing exercises such as making the exhalation longer than the inhalation, which stimulates the relaxation response.

☐ Embodying a sense of peace by, for example, bringing your hands onto your heart momentarily while taking a long, deep breath.

☐ Repetition of a mantra. This might be a chosen word or phrase that brings you a sense of peace and calm.

☐ Writing in a gratitude journal, listing all the things about which you feel grateful and positive, however small these things might seem, for example, 'I am

---

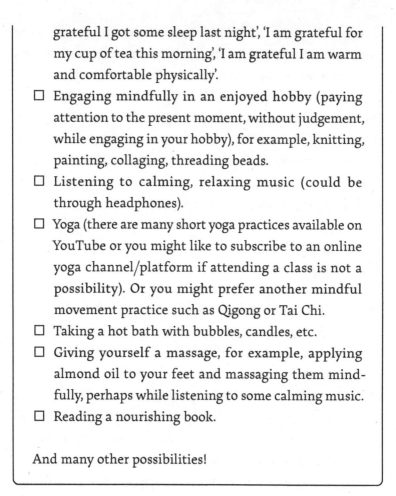

grateful I got some sleep last night', 'I am grateful for my cup of tea this morning', 'I am grateful I am warm and comfortable physically'.

☐ Engaging mindfully in an enjoyed hobby (paying attention to the present moment, without judgement, while engaging in your hobby), for example, knitting, painting, collaging, threading beads.

☐ Listening to calming, relaxing music (could be through headphones).

☐ Yoga (there are many short yoga practices available on YouTube or you might like to subscribe to an online yoga channel/platform if attending a class is not a possibility). Or you might prefer another mindful movement practice such as Qigong or Tai Chi.

☐ Taking a hot bath with bubbles, candles, etc.

☐ Giving yourself a massage, for example, applying almond oil to your feet and massaging them mindfully, perhaps while listening to some calming music.

☐ Reading a nourishing book.

And many other possibilities!

Taking this time for yourself is an opportunity for you to connect to your deeper self, your true self, before engaging in your role as parent, carer and so on. It is likely to help you to become centred in your 'heart' (rather than operating solely from the 'head'). This may make it easier to make an empathetic and relational connection with your child despite the many challenges presenting themselves. If it doesn't feel possible to find 20 minutes – any time is better than no time at all, of course, and even five minutes can be tremendously beneficial! Returning to loved but 'put aside' hobbies can have multiple benefits, including demonstrating to your child an effective way of deriving enjoyment from life, and experiencing a self beyond one's distress and struggles. Sometimes we can tell ourselves that we do not have time for hobbies, particularly if we are caring for a child experiencing emotional distress. However, we can all make time for hobbies, even if this is just for ten minutes a day.

Work and/or volunteering

Sometimes parents tell us that they have had to cut down on their work hours, temporarily give up work or even give up work completely on account of their child's struggles with BDD. Work is a place where many of us find and experience a sense of self outside of the family, which can be particularly important during times of emotional intensity and family difficulty. Work also tends to provide some clear structure to our day and week. For these reasons, re-engaging with work or volunteering can be a very positive and rewarding experience, and you might even be able to link this to your hobbies and interests somehow. Think outside of the box and consider how much time you can realistically give each week (or fortnight or month, if weekly volunteering doesn't feel feasible) and where it might bring you the most joy to spend this time. Organizations such as Do-it.org and NCVO.org can help you to identify voluntary placements in your local area.

While it can be challenging to find someone to look after your child for a full working day, or even to feel safe and happy to do so, it may be possible to find a couple of hours in the week, fortnight or month where your child can be supported by a family member or friend, etc.

Building a support team (including asking for help)

Caring for a child with BDD can feel lonely at times. On top of all the usual struggles of looking after a child with mental health difficulties, you might also be faced with the fact that many people simply haven't heard of BDD and lack understanding of what your child, and indeed the whole family, are dealing with and going through. You might find yourself needing to explain what BDD is to family and friends before you feel able to ask for help from them.

You might like to use the following 'script' as a starting point for explaining something about the experience of BDD to others:

Describing BDD to family, friends and others
Jane is struggling with her mental and emotional health at the moment. She has been diagnosed with something called Body Dysmorphic Disorder, or BDD for short. BDD is actually relatively common in young people of Jane's age, but many people haven't heard of it somehow. It is a mental health diagnosis where the person believes they have defects or flaws in their appearance, and these perceived defects cause them a huge amount of distress.

Jane is really struggling with low self-esteem and feelings of low self-worth right now. These feelings have become focused on Jane's appearance, which is why she was diagnosed with BDD specifically. It has been very difficult for Jane to deal with this, and very difficult for us as a family also. BDD is a very complex and perplexing thing to understand.

I am telling you all of this because I would really appreciate your help and support at this time. To be honest with you, we don't really need advice, as well-meaning as this might be, especially advice about what we should say to Jane, as many of the seemingly logical and helpful things to say are not actually that helpful with BDD. What I would really appreciate would be the opportunity to chat with you from time to time/you being able to look after Jane for a couple of hours each week while I go to my yoga class/etc.

Asking for help can bring up a lot for parents, not least feelings that you *should* be able to manage yourselves, that you *should* know the right thing to say and do in every situation and so on. We warmly urge you to let all of those *shoulds* go. BDD is an incredibly complex experience to navigate and most families will need help in some form or another. Reaching out for help, and asking for support, are actually signs of tremendous strength, resilience and courage.

It can be helpful to draw up a list of trusted people in your life (who you sense are not currently overwhelmed with their own emotions or experiences), who you could potentially reach out to for support. Telephone and face-to-face conversations (or even written letters) can sometimes work better than emails, as people's inboxes are so often bombarded these days. It can also help to be very specific about the kind of support you would ideally like. Reaching out in a vague way can leave people feeling uncertain of how to help, which can sometimes mean that nothing is offered. Don't be afraid of stating exactly what would be most helpful, while communicating that there is not any expectation or obligation. Let the person know you have others you can reach out to if they are not available or able to help if this is the case. Sometimes the type of help you need can be quite simple, like asking a friend to ring you once a fortnight on a Sunday evening to give you a chance to talk through how things are going.

Managing your anxieties

Taking care of a child with BDD can bring a lot of anxieties up for parents, and understandably so. It might be that you require your own psychosocial support (such as counselling) to manage these anxieties. Whether you choose to access your own psychosocial support or not, we hope the following activities may prove to be beneficial.

The Responsibility Pie

Anxieties can often stem from an inflated sense of responsibility and self-blame. Sadly, many parents tie themselves up into knots over what they feel they should be doing to support their child, taking all of the burden and responsibility upon themselves. This is neither healthy nor sustainable. Drawing out a Responsibility Pie can help to put things into perspective, and also support you in identifying where others could step in and be a source of support.

Begin by taking a clean sheet of paper and drawing a large circle. Write the aspect you are feeling anxious about at the top of the page, for example *anxiety about Susie not attending school*. Now think about who holds responsibility in this situation. For example, it might be that the following people hold some part of the responsibility for Susie's low attendance and also for Susie returning to school:

- Susie.
- Yourself as Susie's parent(s).
- School attendance officer.
- School inclusion manager.
- Clinical support team (e.g. clinical psychologist).
- Educational psychologist.

Now apportion a percentage of the 'pie' depending on how much responsibility you believe each person holds. Try to be as objective as possible, perhaps consulting with your partner or a friend to see if your proposed proportions 'check out' with their view of reality. You might like to try this activity with your child (depending on their age and emotional capacity) or to check it out with them after you have had a go.

It can really help to see a visual representation of all those who hold responsibility for that about which you are feeling anxious. It can be a relief to see that you are not alone in this experience and not the only one who is 'supposed' to 'fix' it. The next step might be to call a meeting of everyone within the

Pie to openly discuss the issue and collaboratively agree on ways forward.

Scaling

It can be quite easy to slip into catastrophizing when caring for a young person with BDD. Scaling each catastrophizing thought or feeling can highlight areas of progress and bring the true extent of the current catastrophe to light. Returning to our example, there might be a fear that your child will never be able to return to school. Write this fear down and, underneath it, draw up a scale from 0 to 10, with 0 being that you are absolutely certain they will never return to school and 10 being that you feel they will certainly return to school. Circle the number you feel, pragmatically and objectively, the situation is currently at, taking as many aspects into account as possible, for example, support available, your child's previous school attendance, other young people with BDD you know have returned to school, etc. Let us suppose, for example, that you circle the number 4. Take some time, then, to consider why you did not circle a 3, or even a 2 or a 1. Now consider why you didn't circle a 5 or 6. Reflect upon what would need to happen in order to move the scale up to a 5 or 6. From here, you can talk to the clinical team, and perhaps to your child, about how these aspects could be further supported.

Riding uncertainty

Perhaps the biggest trigger of anxiety and worry in parents is the huge amount of uncertainty BDD brings up. Many parents are desperate to come up with a solution to their child's BDD in order to make things feel more certain and contained.

The difficult truth is that uncertainty and BDD go hand in hand, given the very nature of BDD. Part of managing anxiety, therefore, is increasing your ability to live with uncertainty. Moving through these steps may support you:

- *Weigh the pros and cons of accepting uncertainty.* Identify the ways in which fighting uncertainty is ineffective (cons), and then consider how 'trying to fix things' helps you to feel safe (pros).
- *Identify the times or areas in/of your life where you have/are accepting uncertainty.* There will already be areas of your life in which you both live with and accept uncertainty. These might be experiences like driving to unknown places, navigating traffic jams, waiting for news from a friend, etc. Take some time to consider how accepting some degree of uncertainty is helpful in these situations. Consider how it might be possible to take the same attitude, to a degree, with your child, accepting that you will probably feel uncertain for a while about when they might be returning to school or when they might recover from BDD, for example.
- *Consider what underlying meanings uncertainty may have for you.* Often, uncertainty can be unconsciously associated with negative outcomes. Experiment with taking a step back from this thinking pattern and consider whether there is any evidence for this. Consider all the evidence against this assumption, perhaps recalling times in your life when uncertainty has led to a positive outcome. Just because you feel uncertain about when or whether your

child will return to school, for example, doesn't mean that it will not happen.

- *Imagine a life without uncertainty*. Imagine how it would be if you were certain of everything in relation to your child and their BDD. Consider how closed-off this may lead you to be in terms of their current experience, for example, demonstrating less patience with their refusal to go to school because you are certain they will go back to school at some point. Consider how uncertainty brings with it the possibility of pleasant surprises. Many parents of children with BDD have told us about times when their child has massively surprised them, suddenly coming down from their bedroom in a new outfit (having worn the same outfit for months) or deciding to go into school one day, having refused for an extended period of time.

Parent support groups

Parent support groups can alleviate a sense of aloneness in your struggles, offer solidarity and provide examples of what other parents have found to be beneficial. Specific support groups for parents of young people with BDD are also available online if there are no face-to-face groups in your area. Please see the BDD Foundation website and the OCD Action website for further details.

CHAPTER 11

Our BDD Journeys

Four Parents' Stories

In this chapter, four parents of young people with BDD share their experiences of having a child with BDD and their journeys so far. Three of the four parents are now at the other side of treatment and the child of the other is about to start treatment for BDD. In this chapter, these parents kindly and courageously share their advice on managing day-to-day life when a child has BDD as well as how to navigate through the system of getting a diagnosis and treatment.

Lucy – waiting for treatment

We recognized that our daughter Kirsty had BDD quite quickly. We found the BDD Foundation website and what was described fitted with what Kirsty was experiencing. Our initial referral to CAMHS was dismissed as 'normal teenage behaviour'. We drew the attention of CAMHS clinicians to the BDD Foundation and other information on BDD. Eventually, Kirsty received a diagnosis. She was resistant to accepting the diagnosis of BDD and it took a year for her to accept the label. Initially we tried to reassure her that she was beautiful but after reading about the condition we stopped reassuring her in this way. Instead, we focused on being empathetic and understanding, for example, recognizing trigger situations and accepting that she was in distress.

Our experience has been that family and friends often don't understand. They have seen Kirsty's behaviour, and our accommodation of it, as the problem. It has been very hard to handle these judgements and we have had to be very strong in continuing to believe we are best placed to understand Kirsty's BDD. In practice what we say to family and friends is:

> 'BDD is an anxiety condition, like anorexia, but for BDD the anxiety is focused on Kirsty's perception that she is ugly. Please don't comment on Kirsty's looks. I know this makes it hard to think of things to say, but just be loving and kind.'

BDD has had an impact on the other siblings and the whole family has suffered. There isn't much we have been able to do to prevent this but recognizing and validating the suffering has been important. We have tried to focus on the other children's needs as well as Kirsty's. We have maintained our hobbies and relationships with friends, as a way of making sure we are looking after ourselves. We have also allowed ourselves not to be okay and to recognize that this situation is at times unbearably hard and has had a devastating effect on our lives and relationships.

By being kind to ourselves and recognizing the challenges BDD brings, we have been able to be more resilient and resourceful and not to blame Kirsty. In particular, we have recognized and acknowledged the loss we have experienced when we have seen our daughter suffering to such an extent that she missed a whole year of schooling and wasn't able to engage in the world.

We have experienced many suicide attempts; these have often been preceded by a trigger and we continue to try to be alert to these, and to be in tune with Kirsty's moods and feelings. Our ongoing focus is on empathy and understanding. We regularly ask Kirsty if she is feeling safe and show concern for her safety. We have felt so desperate ourselves that we have been really low and have been referred for counselling.

Kirsty's BDD has made her very reluctant to engage in treatment or medication. She hasn't been ready to engage in CBT (ERP) treatment due to the severity of her condition, but we were willing to try medication, given the impact BDD was having on her life. Of course, we didn't want our daughter to be on medication, but we thought it was better than the risks of what might happen if she was not (although being on medication doesn't reduce all risk, of course). Kirsty now tells us that she feels the medication helps her.

At the moment, we are waiting for CBT through the NHS at a specialist BDD clinic. We feel hopeful that when we are in treatment, things will get better. We can see that things are moving forward, albeit at a slow pace and one we cannot control. While waiting for treatment, our advice to parents would be to become familiar with BDD and the treatment options available through reading books and looking at accredited websites like the BDD Foundation and OCD Action. We also recommend networking with other parents through webinars and conferences.

Here are some more of the things we have learned along the way and some more pointers/advice for you to consider. I hope they are helpful:

- ☐ It is important not to feed into the BDD preoccupations and behaviours (e.g. offering reassurance, running around getting make-up, etc.).
- ☐ Try not to focus on the BDD symptoms (e.g. refrain from commenting on make-up, etc.).
- ☐ The importance of being compassionate and understanding always cannot be over-emphasized. Any sort of disapproval from us has resulted in our daughter internalizing the sense of shame and blame.
- ☐ Your child may misinterpret your meanings and intentions even when you are not being critical (e.g. my daughter became aggressive when I offered her a stress ball).
- ☐ It is important to always avoid being critical of your child and their behaviours in any way.
- ☐ Any challenges should be made gently, and any goals set should be realistic. Be aware that challenges can lead to aggression and/or your child shutting down.
- ☐ We have replaced challenges with expressions of support when our daughter has been particularly struggling.
- ☐ Don't take other people's advice and judgement if you don't think it is informed by an understanding of BDD.
- ☐ Provide a united front if there are two parents present in the household.

Positive things we have done to support our daughter:

- ☐ Building Kirsty's self-esteem through recording things she has done well each day in a notebook.
- ☐ Building positive behaviours (e.g. yoga poses, preparing meals together).

- ☐ Helping Kirsty to develop her understanding of BDD, including helping her to identify her triggers and using this language with her.
- ☐ Keeping positive, no matter what.
- ☐ Not showing disappointment when Kirsty can't do things.

Frances – looking back after treatment

My daughter was diagnosed with BDD when she was 12 years old. She was severely depressed, suicidal, bulimic and was seriously self-harming – we had four visits to A&E. I was in the blackest, darkest place with my daughter and it was really hard sometimes to imagine things would ever get any better.

BUT my daughter is now sociable, kind, empathetic, enjoying life and looking forward to further study. Miracles really can happen! I honestly cannot believe how much progress my daughter has made and think it is really important to share real life positive stories with other parents to demonstrate that anything is possible.

I would say that to access support it is important to persevere with your GP. Look at the BDD Foundation website regarding symptoms so you understand as much as possible. If you think your child may be suffering from BDD, ask your GP about it and then ask what support is available. Don't give up! When speaking to your child about BDD: listen, listen, listen! Never judge and don't offer your opinions or solutions. Ask open questions to help them to see what is going on.

I also recommend asking family members to look at the BDD Foundation website so they can understand what your child and family are experiencing. It has helped us to keep things simple in explanations to the people we trust. We tend to say that BDD is a preoccupation with appearance to the extent that it impacts on life – that's it! We explain that BDD is very common. We ask our friends and extended family members never to comment within earshot of our daughter on anything at all to do with appearance. Even saying, 'You look good in that dress' or, 'You are looking very pretty' can backfire.

There may be times when your child's suffering may be so great that they lash out and say really horrible things, DO NOT take what they say personally. The hideousness of what they say reflects how they feel about themselves; you just happen to be nearby and they clearly feel safe enough with you to express these feelings in your presence. At least your child is expressing feelings rather than bottling them up inside.

I would really recommend that you make sure you do things for you and be gentle with yourself. You will be doing a really good job even if it doesn't feel like it, so just keep going. Don't regret things or the ways you reacted in the past. Don't think that BDD is your fault because it really isn't. Be really proud of yourself for any little results. Remember, you are on a different path to other parents so comparing yourself to other families is unlikely to be helpful at all.

Scarlett – a story of recovery

My daughter started her struggles with BDD in 2010 and over the first few years was misdiagnosed by various professionals. Eventually she put the following search into the internet, 'I am so ugly, I want to die' and found some links to documentaries and websites about BDD. Although my daughter instantly recognized that all the symptoms were very similar to her struggles, she still thought she did not have BDD but was genuinely ugly.

It is very difficult to speak to your child about BDD as, at first, they may not even believe they really have it. They may think they are really ugly and flawed, and might even want to have plastic surgery. They may get angry with you for not believing them and may assume you are against them. They are likely to feel very helpless and frustrated. Conversations were very difficult with my daughter in the early stages and we ended up fighting a lot. We sometimes had arguments that spiralled out of control and my daughter even got physical at times, only then to be really sorry and apologetic later, making her feel worse and terribly guilty. I knew this aggression was so out of character for my daughter, that it was not really her at all – it was the BDD monster that had come to haunt her. I used to blame myself for saying the wrong things or doing something wrong. I now know better and understand that no matter what I said or did, it would not have been the right thing. It is important to let your child know that you understand they are struggling and to remind them regularly that you are there for them. They are likely to need a lot of support in trying to overcome their BDD.

In my experience, it is very difficult to make people truly understand what BDD sufferers are going through. BDD put a huge strain on our family and I had internalized the message that parents are meant to fix things for their children. I constantly felt like I was failing my daughter as I felt so helpless and hopeless.

At the time we were going through the height of my

daughter's BDD struggles, there was a lot of tension in the house including anger, resentment and low moods. BDD got in the way of my daughter's education as she could not make it into school. She wanted nothing more than to go to school and to do normal teenage things, but was unable to do so on account of her BDD. My advice would be not to blame yourself for any of this. You need to take time out for yourself as it is very exhausting looking after someone with BDD.

The first step you will likely need to take is to try and get some help through your GP. This might involve a referral to mental health services like CAMHS. However, be prepared. GPS and CAMHS clinicians are not always aware of BDD. You may have to be persistent to get the right help. The BDD Foundation website has a wealth of information on BDD and where to get help.

My daughter eventually got diagnosed with BDD after three years of struggling including self-harm, suicidal attempts and being housebound. I accompanied my daughter to therapy. She needed a lot of encouragement to go and she was extremely exhausted after each session. It is important to understand that the whole BDD recovery process goes in stages and sometimes young people go backwards a few steps before moving forwards. This made me paranoid, at times, as I was so scared of ending up back at the beginning: at square one. Eventually, I learned to accept that there are good days and bad days. Recovery may be a long process, but it will absolutely be worth all the effort in the end.

My daughter has now completed her undergraduate degree and is about to begin her Masters studies with a view to fulfilling her dream to become a psychologist. She socializes with her friends and has a full and interesting life. My daughter has really turned things around and I want you to know that this is absolutely also a possibility for your child.

Jennie – the importance of hope and love

My son began to show signs of BDD in his junior school days. He had a perfectionist streak and could spot the slightest damage on things. If something wasn't perfect, it upset him a lot. I didn't handle his distress well and often felt both frustrated and angry in response. Back then I didn't realize how much he was battling with anxiety or how bad things could become. I didn't look deeply into why my son was experiencing such anxiety. Mental health issues were something that happened to other families.

Things got worse when my son went to senior school. Here he was cast into an environment where bullying was commonplace. Despite battling with the school in an attempt to force them to take responsibility for my son's safety, they did little more than pay lip service to the prevention of violence. Every day I felt fear about what my son would experience during the school day, and a measure of rage and impotence that he and others were subjected to inadequate provisions made for vulnerable students.

When my son went into puberty he started to exhibit more anxious traits. His clothes and hair had to be perfect, it took ages for him to prepare for school and, again, I often responded to this with little empathy. There were times when I shouted at him in a desperate attempt to get him and his sister to school on time. Gradually I learned that my emotions fed into my son's emotions and vice versa. I began to respond to his anxiety by taking responsibility away from him. I used to feel like his personal valet on school days: everything was set up perfectly so that we could get out without distress.

My son's schooling began to suffer badly and gradually BDD set in. At first, I didn't recognize it. Indeed, back then it was a barely recognized issue and my son was in denial about it. I realized we had a big problem when he completed his GCSEs and the behaviours continued through the summer. Despite the fact that I'm a counsellor myself, I got caught up in giving him reassurance which was an unhelpful but compulsive process which continued for years.

My son limped through his A-levels, barely attending school and then had two failed attempts at attending university. He would say that he lost ten years of his life to BDD. Much of his time was spent with a distorted body clock as he felt it was better to be awake when the rest of the household was asleep. For several years, in fact, he barely left his room. He had a lot of therapy, both CBT (privately and on the NHS) and all kinds of other therapies. This spanned several years.

Living with a person who suffers with BDD can make you feel like you are going mad. I certainly felt that way and on occasions I contemplated suicide myself because my life, my son's life and that of my husband and daughter were all so impacted by the demands of BDD. I took my son for many therapies. Some were good, but no one seemed to understand what my son was going through and they couldn't break the cycle he was caught in. On top of this, he and I also got caught up in the destructive cycle of trying to fix his appearance. Despite the fact that I knew that he was a good-looking young man, his determination was often able to over-ride my reason; so we went for multiple cosmetic appointments such as laser therapy and sought a large array of skin creams and treatments.

Eventually my son was offered a 12-week residential placement at the Anxiety Disorders Residential Unit (ADRU), the national centre of excellence for OCD and BDD in the UK. It was here that, for the first time, my son met others who had the same kind of issues. This was a significant step in enabling him to see that maybe he was suffering with a psychological and not a physical issue. I am grateful to his therapist who suggested he should live independently. However, after he left the hospital, things actually got much worse for a while. There were a number of close encounters with suicide and it was an indescribably awful time for our family.

My son started seeing a therapist who, although not an expert in BDD nor a CBT practitioner, gave him support and encouragement to make some changes in his life. This therapy continued weekly for three years. Gradually things improved as he took hugely courageous steps towards building the life he wanted. These steps led towards a point where he was able to have relationships, live independently and to understand the reasons why he had experienced BDD.

My son went to university and gained an MA in psychology. He wrote his dissertation on the experience of BDD from a psychospiritual perspective. He now works as a coach and therapist supporting other people who are suffering as he once was.

I have learned so much from this journey. Observing my son's battle with BDD has been life changing and has hugely influenced my personal development and my work as a therapist. I am immensely proud of the man my son has become. I couldn't possibly have imagined that one day my son, who was shut away in his bedroom or at death's door, would stand in front of an audience of other therapists and tell his story, that he would be free to search for love and be so strong and compassionate in his work with others.

To other parents I would say: have hope; take responsibility for your own behaviours; notice how your moods may be transmitted to your child; be patient; and, more than anything else, remember that BDD is a symptom of your child's anxiety. Never forget that love is the most important thing in your child's recovery.

CHAPTER 12

Living Life Beyond BDD

This chapter will explore how you can support your child to build an identity outside of and beyond their experience of BDD. It considers how you might talk about the future with your child and how to deal with any setbacks that might arise along the way.

BDD, including recovery from BDD, is typically a journey of many ups and downs, and highs and lows, for the whole family. Some young people respond very well to their first experience of treatment and go on to live a life of being able to manage, or even move completely beyond, their BDD within a relatively short space of time. For other young people, they may need a few rounds of treatment and/or to trial different treatment options and approaches.

As we have discussed, BDD most typically emerges in adolescence. Adolescence is generally a tricky period of life for most of us, partially because it is a critical stage in the development of identity. Adolescents tend to develop an autonomous and integrated self through 'trying themselves out' within different personas, for example, experimenting with different fashion styles, political beliefs, music tastes and so on. A key area of exploration is that of appearance and body image, which becomes the main area of exploration (and distress) in BDD.

BDD can be so 'sticky' because the young person often deeply believes that their appearance is the most important aspect of their identity. To move beyond BDD is, in part, to have:

- Recognized that one has an identity outside of and beyond one's appearance.
- Recognized that BDD is something one is experiencing at the moment; it is not who one *is*.
- Recognized that one is good and lovable, regardless of how one looks.

If a young person has been entrenched in BDD-related preoccupations and behaviours for any period of time, it can be challenging to re-find a self beyond these experiences. It can sometimes also be challenging as a parent to remember and return to the sense of who your child is outside of their BDD, particularly if the BDD has become all-consuming. This is nothing to feel guilty about and could simply be perceived as an invitation to an exploration of your child's core self: their true self. Re-finding your true self also (outside of the identity of being a parent of a young person struggling with BDD) will be important also. This means returning to put-aside desires, passions and hobbies; re-engaging in social and educational/career-related life; and re-connecting with what makes your child (and yourself and other members of the family) feel most invigorated and alive.

You might like to support your child to create a Vision Board for themselves, and/or maybe inspire them by creating your own! A Vision Board is a large piece of card, a cork board or similar filled with images and items which capture one's dreams and desires for the future. Having family members sit together and create their own Vision Boards while listening to music, sharing snacks, etc. can be a lovely way to spend an afternoon. Some people, however, prefer to create their board alone and over a longer period of time.

Emphasizing a growth mindset approach with your child

BDD is very much a fixed mindset experience. What we mean by that is a young person experiencing BDD will feel very 'stuck' in their thoughts and belief systems and have a sense that their abilities and patterns are fixed. On the other side of the spectrum is a *growth mindset* approach. The growth mindset approach, as developed by psychologist Carol Dweck[1] (2017), emphasizes the fact that new abilities, talents, cognitions and ways of looking at the self and the world can develop at any time. Recovery from BDD is, in one sense, a movement from a 'fixed' to a 'growth' mindset, bringing with it the possibility of new and exciting directions and ways of being.

A growth mindset approach emphasizes praise (both given by others and given to the self internally) for effort, persistence, practice, learning from mistakes and progress, as opposed to praise for fixed abilities and outcomes. It acknowledges that we grow through the process of repeatedly falling down, dusting ourselves off and starting over again, and celebrates this

---

1   See www.mindsetworks.com/science.

very process. This means actively commending your child for surviving their slip-backs and promoting these 'mistakes' as opportunities for further growth beyond the narrow confines of BDD.

A growth mindset approach acknowledges and expounds the power of the word 'yet'. Some useful phrases when supporting your child to hold the possibility of their growth in mind, for example, could include:

- ☐ That's right. You can't do it *yet*. If you keep trying, I know you will!
- ☐ Yes, you don't quite understand this aspect of BDD *yet*. If you keep reflecting on it and talking about it, I know you will come to understand it.
- ☐ I know we haven't quite managed to uncover all the mirrors in the house *yet*. Nevertheless, I really feel we are getting there.

Some useful questions you could ask your child to support a growth mindset approach to their recovery from BDD include:

- ☐ What did you do today that made you think about things in a different way?
- ☐ What new strategies did you try today?
- ☐ What mistake did you make today that taught you something?
- ☐ How did you challenge yourself today?

Other growth mindset activities you might like to support your child with include the suggestions in the box on the following page.

Growth mindset-based ideas
to try with your child

☐ Create positive affirmations together, and perhaps write them down and display them in the bedroom or elsewhere, for example, 'I am strong', 'I have unique gifts and talents', 'I am creative', 'I am courageous for trying'.

☐ Encourage your child to write a letter to their current self from their future self (perhaps their ten-years-older-from-now self) offering advice on how to grow towards their dreams.

☐ Make Interest Maps. These are a bit like mind-maps. The young person places an avid interest or passion in the centre (e.g. art) and then maps all related possibilities to this interest, mind-map style.

☐ Encourage your child to interview trusted others about themselves, for example, 'What are my greatest strengths?' 'What do you most appreciate about me?' 'What do you see me doing one/five/ten years from now?'

☐ Support your child to create an Awesome Jar. Encourage your child to decorate a jar and display it somewhere prominent, perhaps in their bedroom. Then encourage them to write down each time they do something towards their passions, vision or goals on a slip of paper and place it into the jar. A Success Journal could be an alternative, perhaps particularly for older young people.

☐ Encourage your child to collect inspirational quotes, postcards, etc. and to display them somewhere visible, perhaps on their Vision Board.

Helping your child to reflect on their experiences with others

Part of moving beyond BDD is returning to school, hobbies, socializing and so on. This can be daunting for young people, particularly if they have been 'out of the loop' for some time. They may have a sense that they need to catch up with school-work, with changes and developments in their social groups, etc. They may also be faced with questions about why they have been away and have not been in touch with their peers.

It can be helpful to sit down with your child for a conversation about the likelihood that people will be naturally curious about why they have been away or have been behaving differently in recent times. Inform your child that some people might ask them questions like, 'Where have you been?' or, 'What have you been doing while you haven't been at school?' It can be helpful to come up with a list of possible questions with your child, and to write down possible responses together, perhaps in collaboration with their therapist.

The amount your child chooses to reveal may be different to different people. Some young people choose to say they have been struggling with BDD and feel able to explain it, and to answer questions about it. Others prefer to be vaguer, perhaps to mention they have been struggling with their mental health or that they have been experiencing a lot of anxiety. Others feel uncomfortable talking about mental health and might choose to say something like, 'I have been working on some stuff, which I don't want to share too much about. I'm glad to be back and I would prefer it if you don't ask me any more questions right now. It is good to see you and I would love to hear about how you are and what's been going on while I've been away!'

Be ready to support your child if they are asked difficult and insensitive questions, reminding them that other people are generally ignorant about BDD and can say things out of a lack of knowledge and understanding. If your child does feel ready to share something about their experience of BDD with friends and family members, you can help them by finding and printing off resources from reputable sources like the BDD Foundation and OCD Action to share with others and by allowing your child to practise such conversations with you beforehand.

Helping your child to navigate an appearance-focused world

Perhaps one of the most difficult aspects of recovering from BDD is that young people are recovering into a world which itself is disordered in terms of appearance expectations and messages. Young people typically continue to be bombarded with homogenous images of 'beauty', to be exposed to a barrage of advertising for products to 'fix' and amend aspects of the appearance, and to be sold the message that belonging, success and lovability are synonymous with how a person looks. This can be a very challenging reality to navigate. The young person must somehow find a resolution between the message they received in therapy – that one must let the distressing focus on the appearance go – and the message received from society – that human beings *should* be focused on the appearance and strive to look a certain way.

Acknowledging this dichotomy with your child is an important step, and an aspect that will also, we hope, have been considered within any therapy they have received. The dilemma is, sadly, likely to keep rearing its head, igniting an ongoing invitation to challenge societal notions of lovability and acceptability wherever possible, as often as is required. You can support your child in this endeavour by returning to the advice outlined in Chapter 9 and by:

- ☐ Helping your child to carefully consider their use of social media, including which Instagram accounts they follow, etc. It might be an idea to sit down with your child for half an hour or so, perhaps over a mug of hot chocolate, and seek positive social media accounts they would like to follow in place of any that might be detrimental to their recovery, for example, removing a dermatologist's account and replacing it with an account linked to a hobby or area of interest outside of appearance. There is quite a body positivity movement now emerging, which is being reflected in the growing number of social media accounts dedicated to this area.
- ☐ Considering what you consume in the family home in terms of what you watch on the television, what magazines you buy, what products you purchase and what messages this might be communicating, for example, anti-wrinkle creams, protein powders, health magazines, etc.
- ☐ Considering how societal messages of beauty impact on your behaviour personally and what this might be communicating to your child, for example, your own endorsement of the dieting culture through subtle choices you make, like buying low-fat everything.

- ☐ Sensitively bringing conversations to a close that involve the regurgitation of societal messages of 'beauty' by others, for example, explaining to a visitor that you respect their decision to go on a diet, but that you prefer not to talk about diets in your household.
- ☐ Having regular, open, non-judgemental conversations with your child about how any societal messages around appearance might be affecting them.
- ☐ Becoming involved, and supporting your child to become involved, in campaigns which challenge societal views of 'beauty'. You might like to write to beauty product companies together, for example, explaining why you would appreciate a different tack taken in their advertising and so on.
- ☐ Regularly engaging with your child in activities that celebrate the function of the body over its form, or inviting them along to activities you enjoy. It can be very powerful for your child to see you wearing your swimming costume with pride and confidence, for example.
- ☐ Reflect a diversity of body types in your home environment through the art and photographs on your walls, the magazines you leave lying around and so on.

Maintaining future-related hope outside of the BDD

Making plans for the future is a really important aspect of recovery from BDD. This is likely to include holding on to hope for the future for your child even when they cannot feel this hope for themselves. As we have mentioned in other chapters, having achievable short and long-term goals can be really beneficial. As one young person shared with us:

> 'It is really important for me to have goals. I think had I not had those goals I have set myself over the years, I would have just given up a long time ago. So, having that sort of future thing to wish for. For me, the thing that kept me going for a while is that I wanted to be a medic one day. Now that has changed. I now want to be a clinical psychologist and to specialize in BDD. I need to have these kinds of hopes and goals for the future as it keeps me going and gives me something to work on. You know, sometimes the BDD can be quite all-consuming, especially when you're in therapy and almost every aspect of what you do is involved in BDD. It is so helpful to have things you think about doing or working on outside of the BDD.'

Having regular chats with your child about their hopes and dreams for the future is very much recommended. It is very important to acknowledge and validate any dreams for the future your child may have, even if they seem rather 'pie in the sky', as to dismiss them could be to reduce the sense of hope your child feels. It is not so necessary to be realistic about future hopes and plans while in the thick of BDD. The most important thing is to have some sort of hope to hang on to. This is not about giving your child 'false hope' but simply about suspending any judgement you have about their dreams for their future outside of the BDD while they are emotionally ill-resourced and struggling. When things have settled down and your child is feeling better, it will be possible to have more pragmatic conversations about what may or may not be possible in terms of academics, career and so on.

Dealing with setbacks

It is important to acknowledge progress each step of the way in your child's journey with BDD. Celebrate the successes, however seemingly small. A journey of a thousand miles always begins with a single step. Acknowledge that BDD is often an undulating journey and there may be setbacks along the way. Sometimes it might feel to the young person as though they are taking three steps forwards and two steps back, or even three steps forward and four steps back. This is all part of the process. Encourage them to keep on putting one foot in front of the other, to 'keep on keeping on'.

Setbacks can be particularly difficult to handle after periods of relative calm or at times when it feels like a significant amount of progress has been made. There can be a sense of, 'but things were going so well'. It can make the whole process of recovery feel exceedingly fragile. While it can feel difficult, and even devastating, at the time, it can be useful to view setbacks as detours. These detours have something positive to offer and can offer new insights and experiences, further embedding the process of recovery and your child's robustness and resiliency. The following case study offers an example of where a setback was an important detour on a young person's recovery journey.

Case study: Peter

Peter had started to attend school for around 50 per cent of his timetable. Peter's mum and dad felt like things were going well and that Peter's personality and zest for life were slowly but surely returning.

Peter came home from school one day in a terrible state. Later that evening, he opened up to his dad, explaining that a kid had made fun of him at school for wearing his baseball cap, which he still wore at lunchtimes regardless of the weather. Peter and his Dad talked through the incident. Peter explained that he felt unable to go to school without the option of his baseball cap, but also could no longer imagine wearing his cap in case he got teased again. He felt confused and afraid.

Peter refused to go to school the next day, and the day after that. Peter's mum and dad began to worry that they were 'back at square one' after so much hard work and encouraging progress.

Peter's parents had an open chat with Peter at the weekend, when the pressure of considering attendance at school was off and Peter was a bit more relaxed. They listened non-judgementally to how uncertain Peter felt about what to do and how ashamed he felt, acknowledging also their feelings of indignation towards the child who had teased Peter. They took time to re-emphasize their ongoing commitment to supporting Peter. Peter was able to share the reasons why he still felt he needed his cap, which centred around fearing his hair being seen in broad daylight.

Peter's mum pulled out some of the worksheets Peter had completed in CBT sessions around his use of the baseball cap, including how Peter could deal with his feelings of panic when he was not wearing it. They remembered together the times that Peter had been out in daylight, including at school, without his cap and how well he had coped at these times. They also talked together about whether people might be more or less likely to notice Peter on account of his hair or on account of his baseball cap. Together, they agreed upon a plan of action based on what Peter had learned in treatment.

The following Monday, Peter rose early and prepared himself for school. His mum fixed his favourite breakfast and spent some time with Peter to go over the plan of action they had agreed together.

As a direct result of this incident, Peter found a way to completely relinquish his use of his baseball cap at school. While it was very painful and difficult, Peter and his family now actually feel a level of gratitude to the boy who teased Peter, as Peter may have resisted facing his fear of going outside in school without his cap for many more months without this unkind but somehow timely prompt.

As we previously highlighted, it can be easy to assume that 'all is lost' and that you are 'back at square one' during times of setback. In reality, a lot of ground has been covered since square one and your child now has a lot more experience, resources and strategies under their belt (as, indeed, do you) to deal with this current setback. Remind yourself of this often, and do not be afraid of reminding your child also. As one young person explained to us:

'One thing that I have noticed is that even though I do still get these downs they never last as long as they used to. And it is easier to come out of them than it used to be. Now I can overcome anxious thoughts much faster.'

Assurances you might like to offer could include:

- ☐ I know things feel a rather tricky again right now, but you have lots of coping strategies you can use like [insert strategy]. I am here to support you and I know we can get through this together.
- ☐ Life is full of ups and downs, isn't it? I'm looking forward to the up that will follow this down, which I feel is just around the corner. Have you noticed how the spring always follows the winter?
- ☐ Things seem quite tough right now, don't they? I keep reminding myself that the tough times never last forever. It can be difficult to remember this during the tough times, can't it? But it is absolutely true.

Using some of the tools offered in Chapter 10 may help you not to catastrophize or panic during times of setback, but rather to view them as further opportunities for growth. We will leave you with some highly insightful and hopeful final reflections from Jennie, the parent who kindly shared the story of her family's journey with BDD in Chapter 11:

Being the parent of a child who suffers can be the loneliest of places. For me there was often an aching longing for normality, the kinds of normality I perceived that others enjoyed. On this journey there can be gut-wrenching, heart-breaking and petrifying moments, hours and days. Sometimes these days turn into weeks and years, our lives becoming consumed in the role of carer, defender, teacher, confidant, friend and parent.

In the impossibility of the situation, we may feel lost, fearful and alone. Complex emotions such as shame, rage, grief, disappointment, resentment, despair, fear and envy may arise, even though we make attempts to stay grounded.

We may be able to set about making sense of all this for ourselves and in so doing be able to take the courageous steps to challenge and perhaps change ourselves in order that we can better support our child's recovery. Even without this kind of introspection, transformation can occur.

I'm not sure that this hope of transformation is any kind of comfort or compensation. Perhaps it is only in retrospect that we can begin to see the ways in which we have grown as a result of the challenging and often desperate situation of caring for a child with BDD. As some parents of children and young people with BDD have told me:

I have transformed into a much more patient person. I had to learn to slow down and take time to care for my child and myself.

I learnt that the trivial things in life that once felt so important are meaningless and often unhelpful.

I was forced to become assertive and sometimes a warrior mother because I had to battle with authority. I became quite a skilful negotiator.

I transformed from being a highly competitive parent to learning that there's no point in concerning myself with the progress of other people's children, nor is there any point in pressuring my child to fit in with 'normal' milestones or for that matter to harass them in any way.

I guess this meant I had to stop being so full of pride and this has been a hard lesson. I used to dream that my child would be a great success; now success is when he has a good day and leaves his room for half an hour.

I have learned to be compassionate to others who have mental health issues. Becoming less judgemental was a big transformation for me. In turn, I learned to be more compassionate with myself and with my children.

I had to ask for help which was something I had previously really struggled with. I found out that other people have similar experiences and that most people are happy to help. It was a bit like learning to fail. It has been hard but something definitely worth facing.

My relationship to my own emotions transformed. I discovered that for years I hadn't managed anger well.

As part of my survival, I learned to meditate. This brought about a big transformation in my life.

I have come to see how resilient, committed, strong and determined I can be.

Glossary of Terms

A&E – Accident and Emergency department of a hospital, sometimes called the Emergency Room.

Attention retraining – Attention retraining describes re-learning how to direct and move the attention towards and away from objects and experiences rather than becoming fixated on singular aspects such as the perceived appearance flaw or defect.

Attuned relationship – An attuned relationship is a relationship within which emotional states are regularly shared and reciprocated, and within which mutual understanding and empathy is present.

BDD – Body dysmorphic disorder.

Bullying – An experience of being repeatedly teased and/or treated unkindly by another or others. This can be physical, verbal, psychological or a combination.

CAMHS – Child and Adolescent Mental Health Services; community-based mental health services for children and young people up to the age of 18 in the UK. Referred to as EWMHS in some areas (Emotional Wellbeing and Mental Health Service).

Camouflage – An attempt to hide a perceived appearance defect or flaw, e.g. with clothing, make-up, etc.

CBT – Cognitive behavioural therapy. A recommended therapy for BDD which addresses thoughts, feelings and behaviours.

Compulsion – Repetitive behaviours or mental acts a person feels driven to perform in response to an obsession (see *Obsession*).

Cosmetic procedure – A procedure undertaken to alter aspects of the appearance through the use of surgery, treatments and/ or products.

Cyber-bullying – Bullying that takes place online (see *Bullying*).

DSM-V – *Diagnostic and Statistical Manual of Mental Disorders (5th Edition)*. A manual used by mental health professionals to diagnose mental health conditions. The other manual used by mental health clinicians is the *International Classification of Diseases*, now in its tenth edition (*ICD-10*).

Dysregulation – Dysregulation refers to an imbalance in the autonomic nervous system which causes the young person to feel hyper-(over) aroused or hypo-(under) aroused physically, emotionally and psychologically.

EHCP – Education, Health and Care Plan. This replaced the Statement of Special Educational Needs in the UK. It is a collaborative plan drawn up by the education and health authorities providing a detailed outline of the needs and barriers for a young person. It comes with the provision of additional funding to meet the young person's needs in their education or work setting and is reviewed annually.

Environmental factors – Factors related to the physical, social, cultural and political environment in which a person lives, e.g. family relationships, financial resources, available community support, etc.

EP – Educational psychologist (sometimes called a school psychologist). A chartered psychologist who specializes in supporting young people in education settings.

ERP – Exposure and Response Prevention (see also separate entries for *Exposure* and for *Response Prevention*). A recommended therapy for BDD (CBT with ERP) that encourages facing one's fears and letting obsessive thoughts occur without 'putting them right' or 'neutralising' them with compulsions.

Exposure – Procedure for gradually facing one's fears in a graded manner.

Family accommodation – How family members alter their behaviour to alleviate the distress of a relative suffering with BDD.

GP – General Practitioner. Also often called a family doctor.

Hierarchy – A technique used within ERP (see *ERP*) where the young person is supported to make a list of feared actions starting with the least feared, working up to the most feared.

Inclusion team – Staff in education settings responsible for ensuring all children, including those with special educational needs and/or emotional/mental health difficulties, are included in school life and can access the curriculum. Many education settings have Inclusion Managers, sometimes referred to as Special Educational Needs Coordinators (SENCo).

Mirror retraining – People with BDD tend to use mirrors and describe their appearance in a negative and unkind way. Mirror retraining refers to re-learning how to use the mirror in a way most people without BDD would use it. It involves helping the young person to change how they look in the mirror. It might include learning to describe themselves in a holistic and non-judgemental way. It also includes reduction in the time spent in front of the mirror, looking into the mirror from further away, giving up using hand-held mirrors for checking the appearance, etc.

Motivational interviewing – A therapeutic approach focused on solutions and future goals.

Muscle dysmorphia – A sub-type of BDD in which there is a distressing preoccupation with one's musculature.

Non-judgemental attitude – Encompasses the attitude of unconditionally holding the self and/or the other person in positive regard without any sense of blame.

Obsession – Recurrent and persistent thoughts, impulses or images that cause distressing emotions such as anxiety or disgust.

OCD – Obsessive compulsive disorder (see also *Compulsion* and *Obsession*). A mental health condition characterized by obsessive thoughts and compulsive behaviours.

Perceived defects/flaws – In BDD, the young person believes they have a genuine flaw or defect in their appearance. As this view is not shared by others, we say it is perceived.

Reassurance seeking – In the context of BDD, an attempt to obtain verbal feedback about a perceived appearance defect or flaw (often repetitive).

Response Prevention – The process of preventing a ritual – for example, not checking in a mirror.

Safety behaviour – In the context of BDD, a behaviour undertaken to hide the perceived defect in an attempt to alleviate feelings of distress and anxiety.

Self-efficacy – To have high self-efficacy is to have a strong sense of one's capacity to exert some control over one's behaviour, emotions and environment.

Social anxiety – Intense fear and worry before, during and after social situations.

Social media – Websites and applications used to create and share content or participate in social networking.

SEN – Special educational need(s). Could be in the areas of cognition and learning; social, emotional and mental health; physical and sensory development; and/or speech, language and social communication.

Specifiers – Specifiers are extensions to a diagnosis to further clarify a condition or illness.

SSRIs – Selective serotonin reuptake inhibitors. A recommended group of anti-depressant medications for BDD.

Trauma – An event in which emotional resources are overwhelmed and there is a limited or absent possibility to fight back or escape in any way.

References

Beilharz, F., Castle, D.J., Grace, S. and Rossell, S.L. (2017). A systematic review of visual processing and associated treatments in body dysmorphic disorder. *Acta Psychiatrica Scandinavica, 136*(1), 16-36.

Bienvenu, O., Samuels, J., Riddle, M., Hoehn-Saric, R. *et al.* (2000). The relationship of obsessive-compulsive disorder to possible spectrum disorders: results from a family study. *Biological Psychiatry, 48*(4), 287–293.

Browne, H.A., Gair, S.L., Scharf, J.M. and Grice, D.E. (2014). Genetics of obsessive-compulsive disorder and related disorders. *Psychiatric Clinics, 37*(3), 319–335.

Buhlmann, U., Marques, L. M. and Wilhelm, S. (2012). Traumatic experiences in individuals with body dysmorphic disorder. *The Journal of Nervous and Mental Disease, 200*(1), 95–98.

Didie, E.R., Tortolani, C.C., Pope, C.G., Menard, W., Fay, C. and Phillips, K.A. (2006). Childhood abuse and neglect in body dysmorphic disorder. *Child Abuse & Neglect, 30*(10), 1105–1115.

Dweck, C. (2017). *Mindset: Changing the Way you Think to Fulfil Your Potential.* London: Robinson Press.

Enander, J., Ivanov, V. Z., Mataix-Cols, D., Kuja-Halkola, *et al.* (2018). Prevalence and heritability of body dysmorphic symptoms in adolescents and young adults: a population-based nationwide twin study. *Psychological Medicine, 48*(16), 2740–2747.

Feusner, J.D., Townsend, J., Bystritsky, A. and Bookheimer, S. (2007). Visual information processing of faces in body dysmorphic disorder. *Archives of General Psychiatry, 64*(12), 1417–1425.

Feusner, J. D., Moody, T., Hembacher, E., Townsend, J., McKinley, M., Moller, H. and Bookheimer, S. (2010). Abnormalities of visual processing and frontostriatal systems in body dysmorphic disorder. *Archives of General Psychiatry, 67*(2), 197–205.

Feusner, J.D., Hembacher, E., Moller, H. and Moody, T.D. (2011). Abnormalities of object visual processing in body dysmorphic disorder. *Psychological Medicine, 41*(11), 2385–2397.

Gilbert, P. (2009). *The Compassionate Mind.* London: Constable.

Gilbert, P. (2010). *Compassion-Focused Therapy.* London: Routledge.

Jefferies, K., Laws, K.R. and Fineberg, N.A. (2012). Superior face recognition in body dysmorphic disorder. *Journal of Obsessive-Compulsive and Related Disorders, 1*(3), 175–179.

López-Solà, C., Fontenelle, L.F., Alonso, P., Cuadras, D. *et al.* (2014). Prevalence and heritability of obsessive-compulsive spectrum and anxiety disorder symptoms: a survey of the Australian Twin Registry. *American Journal of Medical Genetics Part B: Neuropsychiatric Genetics, 165*(4), 314–325.

Marazziti, D., Dell'Osso, L. and Presta, S. (1999). Platelet [3H]paroxetine binding in patients with OCD-related disorders. *Psychiatry Research, 89*(3), 223–228.

Maudsley Hospital National and Specialist OCD, BDD and Related Disorders Service (2019). *Appearance Anxiety: A Guide to Understanding Body Dysmorphic Disorder for Young People, Families and Professionals.* London: Jessica Kingsley Publishers.

Monzani, B., Rijsdijk, F., Anson, M., Iervolino, A.C. *et al.* (2012a). A twin study of body dysmorphic concerns. *Psychological Medicine*, 42(9), 1–7.

Monzani, B., Rijsdijk, F., Iervolino, A.C., Anson, M., Cherkas, L. and Mataix-Cols, D. (2012b). Evidence for a genetic overlap between body dysmorphic concerns and obsessive–compulsive symptoms in an adult female community twin sample. *American Journal of Medical Genetics Part B: Neuropsychiatric Genetics*, 159(4), 376–382.

Monzani, B., Rijsdijk, F., Harris, J. and Mataix-Cols, D. (2014). The structure of genetic and environmental risk factors for dimensional representations of DSM-5 obsessive-compulsive spectrum disorders. *JAMA Psychiatry*, 71(2), 182–189.

National Institute for Health and Cave Excellence (2015). *Treating Obsessive-Compulsive Disorder (OCD) and Body Dysmorphic Disorder (BDD) in Adults, Children and Young People.* Clinical Guidance CG31.

Neff, K. (2011). *Self-Compassion.* London: Yellow Kite.

Neziroglu, F., Khemlani-Patel, S. and Yaryura-Tobias, J.A. (2006). Rates of abuse in body dysmorphic disorder and obsessive-compulsive disorder. *Body Image*, 3(2), 189–193.

Neziroglu, F., Borda, T., Khemlani-Patel, S. and Bonasera, B. (2018). Prevalence of bullying in a pediatric sample of body dysmorphic disorder. *Comprehensive Psychiatry*, 87, 12–16.

Perry, B. (2013). 'Born for Love: The Effects of Empathy on the Developing Brain.' Speech to Annual Interpersonal Neurobiology Conference 'How People Change: Relationship & Neuroplasticity in Psychotherapy', UCLA Extension, Los Angeles, March 8.

Perry, B.D. and Hambrick, E.P. (2008). The Neurosequential Model of Therapeutics. *Reclaiming Children and Youth Magazine*, Fall 2008, Vol 17. Nr 3, www.reclaiming.com, (UCLA handout).

Perry, B.D. and Hambrick, E.P. (2010). *Introduction to the Neurosequential Model of Therapeutics (NMT)*. Houston, TX: Child Trauma Academy.

Weingarden, H., Curley, E.E., Renshaw, K.D. and Wilhelm, S. (2017). Patient-identified events implicated in the development of body dysmorphic disorder. *Body Image, 21,* 19–25.

Resources

A leaflet offering guidance for schools and educational settings supporting young people with BDD can be downloaded at: https://bddfoundation.org/wp-content/uploads/BDD-Leaflet-for-Education-Professionals.pdf.

A card for taking along to GPs and other professionals explaining what BDD is can be downloaded at: https://bddfoundation.org/wp-content/uploads/FINAL-GP-CARD.pdf.

The BDD Foundation have created a short animation about BDD from the perspective of a young person who has recovered. This can be accessed via the BDD Foundation website: https://bddfoundation.org/home-new-animation.

Books

BDD

National and Specialist OCD, BDD and Related Disorders Clinic (2019). *Appearance Anxiety: A Guide to Understanding Body*

Dysmorphic Disorder for Young People, Families and Professionals. London: Jessica Kingsley Publishers.

Phillips, K. (2005). *The Broken Mirror: Understanding and Treating Body Dysmorphic Disorder.* Oxford: Oxford University Press.

Phillips, K. (2009). *Understanding Body Dysmorphic Disorder: An Essential Guide.* Oxford: Oxford University Press.

Pope, H. and Philips, K. (2002). *The Adonis Complex: How to Identify, Treat and Prevent Body Obsession in Men and Boys: The Secret Crisis of Male Body Obsession.* New York: Free Press.

Schnackenberg, N. and Petro, S. (2016). *Reflections on Body Dysmorphic Disorder: Stories of Courage, Determination and Hope.* London: The BDD Foundation.

Veale, D., Willson, R. and Clarke, A. (2009). *Overcoming Body Image Problems Including Body Dysmorphic Disorder.* Quincy, MA: Robinson Press.

Anxiety and social anxiety

Abey, K. (2017). *No Worries! Mindful Kids: An Activity Book for Young People Who Sometimes Feel Anxious or Stressed.* London: Studio Press.

Collins-Donnelly, K. (2013). *Starving the Anxiety Gremlin: A Cognitive Behavioural Therapy Workbook on Managing Anxiety for Young People.* London: Jessica Kingsley Publishers.

Herrick, E. and Redman-White, B. (2018). *Supporting Children and Young People with Anxiety.* London: Routledge.

Fitzpatrick, C. (2015). *A Short Introduction to Helping Young People Manage Anxiety.* London: Jessica Kingsley Publishers.

O'Neill, P. (2018). *Don't Worry, Be Happy: A Child's Guide to Overcoming Anxiety.* New York: Vie Publishing.

Depression

Collins-Donnelly, K. (2019). *Starving the Depression Gremlin: A Cognitive Behavioural Therapy Workbook on Managing Depression for Young People*. London: Jessica Kingsley Publishers.

Fitzpatrick, C. (2004). *Coping with Depression in Young People: A Guide for Parents*. New Jersey: Wiley.

OCD

Chansky, T. (2001). *Freeing Your Child From OCD*. New York: Times Books.

Derisley, J., Heyman, I., Robinson, S. and Turner, C. (2008). *Breaking Free from OCD: A CBT Guide for Young People and Their Families*. London: Jessica Kingsley Publishers.

Huebner, D. and Matthews, B. (2007). *What To Do When Your Brain Gets Stuck: A Kid's Guide to Overcoming OCD*. Washington DC: Magination Press.

Jassi, A. (2013). *Can I Tell You About OCD?* London: Jessica Kingsley Publishers.

Eating disorders

Bryant-Waugh, R. and Lask, B. (2013). *Eating Disorders: A Parents' Guide*. London: Routledge.

Musby, E. (2014). *Anorexia and Other Eating Disorders: How to Help your Child Eat Well and Be Well*. APRICA.

Trichotillomania and skin-picking (excoriation) disorder

Keuthen, N. and Stein, D. (2001). *Help for Hair Pullers: Understanding and Coping with Trichotillomania*. Oakland, California: New Harbinger Publications.

Mansueto, C. (2020). *Overcoming Body-Focused Repetitive Behaviours: A Comprehensive Behavioural Treatment for Hair Pulling and Skin Picking*. Oakland, CA: New Harbinger Publications.

Substance misuse
Bowden-Jones, O. (2016). *The Drug Conversation: How to Talk to Your Child About Drugs*. London: RCPsych Publications.

Self-esteem
Collins-Donnelly, K. (2014). *Banish Your Self-Esteem Thief: A Cognitive Behavioural Therapy Workbook on Building Positive Self-Esteem for Young People*. London: Jessica Kingsley Publishers.

Cope, A. (2014). *The Art of Being a Brilliant Teenager*. North Mantrato MN: Capstone.

O'Neill, P. (2018). *You're a Star: A Child's Guide to Self-Esteem*. New York: Vie Publishing.

Syed, M. and Triumph, T. (2018). *You are Awesome: Find your Confidence and Dare to be Brilliant at (Almost) Anything*. London: Wren and Rook.

Social media
Betton, V. and Woollard, J. (2018). *Teen Mental Health in an Online World: Supporting Young People Around Their Use of Social Media, Apps, Gaming, Texting and the Rest*. London: Jessica Kingsley Publishers.

Saedi Bocci, G. (2019). *The Social Media Workbook for Teens*. Oakland, CA: New Harbinger Publications.

Growth mindset

Dweck, C. (2017). *Mindset: Changing the Way you Think to Fulfil Your Potential*. London: Robinson Press.

Tough, P. (2014). *How Children Succeed: Grit, Curiosity, and the Hidden Power of Character*. London: Arrow.

Siegel, D. and Payne Bryson, T. (2018). *The Yes Brain Child: Help Your Child Be More Resilient, Independent and Creative*. New York: Simon and Schuster.

Useful websites

The BDD Foundation: www.bddfoundation.org

OCD Action: www.ocdaction.org.uk

International OCD Foundation: https://bdd.iocdf.org

Mind UK: www.mind.org.uk

Anxiety UK: www.anxietyuk.org.uk

BEAT Eating Disorders: www.b-eat.co.uk

Bullying UK: www.bullying.co.uk

Childline: www.childline.org.uk

Depression Alliance: www.depressionalliance.org

Family Lives (family and parenting support): www.familylives.org.uk

Papyrus (young suicide prevention) www.papyrus-uk.org

SkinPick (online community for skin picking) www.skinpick.com

Young Minds: www.youngminds.org.uk

Growth mindset
Big Life Journal (for a range of downloadable Growth Mindset Resources): www.biglifejournal.com

Mindset Online (the website of Growth Mindset creator Carol Dweck): www.mindsetworks.com

Crisis helplines

UK
Childline: For help and advice on a range of issues.
www.childline.org.uk
0800 11 11

Papyrus: The UK's leading charity for the prevention of youth suicide.
Hopeline (by Papyrus): A confidential support and advice service for:
Children and young people under the age of 35 who are experiencing thoughts of suicide.
Anyone concerned that a young person could be thinking about suicide.
www.papyrus-uk.org
0800 068 41 41
0778 620 9697
pat@papyrus-uk.org

Samaritans: Confidential 24-hour-a-day crisis line.
116 123
www.samaritans.org
jo@samaritans.org

SANEline: For people experiencing mental health difficulties or those supporting them.
www.sane.org.uk
0300 304 7000

The Mix: For young people under 25 struggling with their mental health.
www.themix.org.uk
0808 808 4994

Young Minds: Offer a parent helpline and young persons' crisis messenger service.
www.youngminds.org.uk
Parent Helpline: 0808 802 5544
Young Persons' Crisis Messenger Service:
Text YM to 85258

US

National Suicide Prevention Lifeline (USA): Provides 24/7, free and confidential support for people in distress and prevention and crisis resources.
1-800-273-8255

United States National Crisis and Suicide Hotlines website
http://suicidehotlines.com/national.html

International OCD Foundation – includes a section on their website about BDD and a resource directory for finding help for BDD
https://bdd.iocdf.org

Mental Health America
www.mhanational.org/childrens-mental-health
Includes a section specifically related to young people: www.mhanational.org/childrens-mental-health – and also a section on BDD: www.mhanational.org/conditions/body-dysmorphic-disorder-bdd.

US-based mental health advice and resources
www.mentalhealth.gov

National Federation of Families for Children's Mental Health
US-based children's mental health advice and resources
www.ffcmh.org

US-based children's mental health portal
www.kidsmentalhealth.org

About the Authors

Dr Nicole Schnackenberg is a child, community and educational psychologist working for the Southend Educational Psychology Service in Essex, UK. She is a trustee of the BDD Foundation and co-facilitates BDD support groups both face to face and online. Nicole's doctoral research was into young people's experiences of BDD, which led to the creation of the Shame-Identity Model of BDD in Young People. Nicole has written and edited previous books about BDD and has lectured internationally on the topic.

Dr Benedetta Monzani is a clinical psychologist at the National Specialist OCD, BDD and Related Disorders Service for young people at the Maudsley Hospital and the clinical advisor for the BDD Foundation. Before completing her doctorate in clinical psychology at the Institute of Psychiatry (King's College London), she completed her PhD at the same institution, examining neuropsychological differences and genetic factors in BDD. Benedetta has gained clinical and research experience with BDD, having trained and worked at various national BDD clinics in the UK and US. Alongside her clinical practice, she continues to be actively involved in writing about, and researching into, BDD, OCD and related disorders. She has published a number of peer-reviewed articles on BDD and hopes to help raise awareness of BDD through teaching, media and research.

Dr Amita Jassi is a consultant clinical psychologist at the National Specialist OCD, BDD and Related Disorders Service for young people at the Maudsley Hospital in London, UK. She leads the BDD branch of the service and has worked with this client group since 2006. Amita is also a trustee of the BDD Foundation. In her clinical role, she develops and delivers individually tailored treatment packages, including intensive, home-based and inpatient treatment, as well as offering consultation and joint work with clinicians around the country. Amita has taught and trained nationally and internationally on child and adolescent BDD. She is the author of several books including *Appearance Anxiety: A Guide to Understanding Body Dysmorphic Disorder for Young People, Families and Professionals*. Amita has published several papers in peer-reviewed journals on BDD and engages in media work to increase awareness and understanding of this under-recognized condition.

Index

treatments, supporting your
    child through
  co-therapist role 138–9
  key facets 141–5
  motivating 140–1
  reducing family
      accommodation 146–9
  refusing treatment 150–2
  relapse prevention 149–50
trichotillomania (hair-pulling
    disorder) 29

uncertainty management
    177–9
universities 110–11
unrealistic appearance ideals
    161

validation 90, 101, 110, 111
video chats 47
Vision Boards 193–4, 196

visual processing differences
    33–4
volunteering, parents 172–3

weight *see* eating disorders
    and BDD
Wilhelm, S. 35
work, parents 172–3
writing
  forms of family
      accommodation 146
  gratitude journal 170–1
  growth mindset activities
      196
  successes 141
  thoughts and feelings 139

Yaryura-Tobias, J.A. 35

Zoom/Skype video chats 47